FIREPROOF YOUR LIFE

BUILDING A FAITH THAT SURVIVES THE FLAMES

MICHAEL CATT

PUBLICATIONS

Fort Washington, PA 19034

• Fireproof Your Life •

Published by CLC Publications

U.S.A.
P.O. Box 1449, Fort Washington, PA 19034

GREAT BRITAIN
51 The Dean, Alresford, Hants. SO24 9BJ

AUSTRALIA
P.O. Box 2299, Strathpine, QLD 4500

NEW ZEALAND
10 MacArthur Street, Feilding

ISBN: 978-0-87508-984-3

Advance praise for

Michael Catt, Sherwood Baptist Church and

Fireproof Your Life

Michael Catt has a message for all of us! Read it and you'll be encouraged in God to face the tumultuous spiritual times we live in. This book will bless your life!

Pastor Jim Cymbala
The Brooklyn Tabernacle

Michael Catt is a dear friend and the kind of servant I hope to be someday—the kind that God loves to bless, because he does not hesitate to pass those blessings on to others. With a deeply generous and honest heart, he shares a lifetime of spiritual truth gained and lived out at the feet of some of God's greatest spiritual men and women. He has lived out these great ideas and knows the most practical way of expressing them in writing. This book brings these rich insights to bear on the subject of preparing your life for the inevitable fires that will come your way. I cannot think of a better way to withstand the test of your life, family and home than to be inspired by *Fireproof Your Life* by Michael Catt.

Ed Litton
Senior Pastor
First Baptist Church of North Mobile
Saraland, AL

Michael Catt has touched a nerve felt by all of us in *Fireproof Your Life*. Dealing with the most obvious challenges of life and relationships, he has shown us how to protect these vital areas. He uses creative illustrations and clear scriptural principles to drive home the point that God wants us to "fireproof" every area of our lives. God's Word is the basis for the strategies presented. This is a great book for everyone who desires to live a life that is protected from the pitfalls and dangers before us. He has lived out these principles and proven them in the fires of his own journey in life.

Jimmy Draper
President Emeritus
LifeWay Christian Resources

Michael Catt demonstrates godly wisdom in every sphere of life. It's the strength of what he practices and his unusual authenticity about why he is teaching and living it that makes these Biblical proclamations so powerful and practical. Follow this blueprint carefully and experience the blessing of God in every area of your life.

James MacDonald
Senior Pastor
Harvest Bible Chapel
Rolling Meadows, IL

To
Terri

The love of my life,
my best friend,
my Georgia peach and
the mother of our two daughters.
You have walked with me through many fires
and prayed for me when I wasn't at my best.
I am a blessed man.

Contents

Acknowledgments

There is no such thing as a self-made man. Anyone who finds some measure of success has done it because of a partnership with others. It is the "others" who have invested in us who make us who we are. Without them we would be limited in our focus, understanding and impact.

Ken Jenkins provided the inspiration for this book. When you read his material in the first chapter, you will understand why. Ken is a *National Geographic* award-winning photographer. He is one of the most godly laymen I have ever known. His photography is second to none. His awareness of God in creation (Romans 1:20) is inspiring. I'm eternally grateful for Ken's willingness to share the story of the sequoias with me for this book.

Without the folks at CLC who first believed in me as an author, I would still be a frustrated writer. They have been incredibly supportive in this process. A special thanks to Dave Almack, Becky English, Dave Fessenden and Jim Pitman for helping with the final edit and adding their expertise. I am grateful for the partnership.

The members of Sherwood Baptist Church, where I've had the privilege of pastoring for nearly twenty years, have prayed for me, encouraged me and, at times, tolerated me. I know without a doubt their prayers have shielded me in and from many fires. The staff frees me up to expand the ministry God has given me. They are my Knights of the Round Table who stand shoulder to shoulder, shield to shield, ready for anything and everything. Special thanks to Jim McBride, my executive pastor, whose tireless support and input keeps pushing me on.

Debbie Toole has been my administrative assistant for nearly eighteen years. Debbie makes sure I'm where I'm supposed to be, when I'm supposed to be there. She's a God-send to me and my ministry. Stephanie Bennett, my research assistant, has helped me pull this material together and has made the initial edits and corrections. Stephanie is diligent in all she does and makes me look like I actually passed my English grammar classes.

My wife, Terri, reminded me of numerous stories and situations that I had forgotten in the first draft. Without her input, this book would be lacking. Our oldest daughter, Erin, is living for Christ as an actress and entertainer for a major entertainment company. She has seen up close and personal the effects of work associates who play with fire. Our youngest daughter, Hayley, was our church photographer on the set of *Fireproof.* Her pictures are on the cover of this book and have been used in numerous publications, including *Outreach Magazine* and *Christianity Today.* You'll also find her pictures on the *Fireproof* website. She's using her photographer's eye to capture images to be used for the glory of God.

Two preachers have invested much in me in recent years. God allowed me to get to know Warren Wiersbe in the mid-1990s, and he has been a constant source of encouragement. His wisdom and insights are invaluable. I never talk to him when I don't have a pen in hand. His nuggets of truth off the top of his head reveal a deep mine full of riches learned at the feet of Jesus. I am listening and learning from one of God's giants.

I have known Tom Elliff for a long time. In recent years, he has become a key adviser, friend and confidant. I've watched him walk through the fires of ministry from a distance and up close. He is a man you would want to walk with through a fire. Tom models for me the Spirit-filled life that can survive life's fires.

I am blessed to have prayer warriors in the church and around the country. These individuals have covered me in ways only eternity will reveal. Paul said it best in his letter to the Philippians: "Yes, and I will rejoice, for I know that this will turn out for my deliverance through your prayers and the provision of the Spirit of Jesus Christ . . ."(1:18–19). We need both. I need both. To live a fireproof life, I am desperate for the prayers of the saints and the provision of the Spirit. I know in glory I will praise God for my deliverance from fires the Enemy set for me because of the prayer that bombarded heaven on my behalf and because of the provisions of the Spirit of Christ.

There are many casualties in the family of God. Some warm themselves at the Enemy's fire, while others play with fire. Many foolishly think they are fireproof in their own strength. This book is written with the prayer that we will all finish well. Although the fires will come, we can make preparations for them. We don't have to be casualties or statistics. We can do more than survive. My prayer for you is that God would use these pages, along with the prayers of the saints and the provisions of the Spirit, to see you safely home.

Michael Catt
Albany, Georgia

There it stands—after being struck by lightning, attacked by fires, stung by wasps and weathered by thousands of snowstorms—resolute above all other trees, distinctive and majestic in its beauty. The branches are eight to ten feet in diameter and thinned out until only a few of the strongest and most strategically placed are held in a dome-like crown.

He will be like a tree firmly
planted by streams of water . . .
(Ps. 1:3)

1

Standing in the Fire

MY FRIEND Ken Jenkins is a professional photographer.[1] The back cover and each chapter of this book feature his sequoia photographs taken several years ago in California. While researching this series of photos, Ken had a lengthy conversation with one of the foresters there.

As the photo shows, there had been a forest fire among these giant trees, some of which are so old they date back to the time of Christ. A sequoia can live through many fires, surviving because its bark is two feet thick. But after a fire, a tree can smolder for six to twelve months from the "pain and suffering" of the flames that lashed at the bark.

When trials by fire come we often find ourselves smoldering. We end up asking God, "Why this?" or "Why me?" We can even buy into the lie: "If God loved me, He wouldn't have allowed this to happen." But it is wrong to assume that God does not love us, does not care or does not know what we are going through.

The reality is that all of us go through fires and times of testing. Trials show what we are made of—they reveal our hearts, our faith, our level of maturity. The fires in the se-

Trials show what we are made of—they reveal our hearts, our faith, our level of maturity.

quoia forests actually produce favorable results: when the cone of the sequoia is burned, it dries out, pops open and disperses its seeds. Experts tell us each cone, though only two and a half inches long and an inch and a half wide, contains up to two hundred seeds. The wind carries the seeds and deposits them on the ground as silently as snowflakes. And so life springs from death and the flames result in new birth.

A Cultivated Heart

Ironically, however, the forest that Ken was photographing contains no young trees. If fire opens a cone which produces two hundred seeds, and one tree can produce tens of thousands of cones, why isn't there new growth? Where are all the young sequoia trees?

Unfortunately, tourists and onlookers have caused another problem: the ground has been hardened by their trampling feet. With no cultivation or breaking up of the soil, the seeds cannot take root and multiply. The key to the growth of the seeds is nitrogen-rich soil, the result of layer upon layer of ash from many fires.

Jesus' parable of the sower holds great truths about fireproofing your life—how to live a life that can withstand the fire and produce fruit.

And He spoke many things to them in parables, saying, "Behold, the sower went out to sow; and as he sowed, some seeds fell beside the road, and the birds came and ate them up. Others fell on the rocky places, where they did not have much soil; and immediately they sprang up, because they had no depth of soil. But when the sun had risen, they were scorched; and because they had no root, they withered away. Others fell among the thorns, and the thorns came up and choked them out. And others fell on the good soil and yielded a crop, some a hundredfold, some sixty, and some thirty. He who has ears, let him hear." (Matt. 13:3–9)

In this parable Jesus is the sower, the Word is the seed and our heart is the soil. We would all agree there is no problem with the sower or the seed. The problem is with the soil—our hearts. We've allowed things to keep us from bearing fruit and growing in godliness.

Read carefully the Master's explanation of the parable. You don't have to be a Greek scholar to figure this out.

Hear then the parable of the sower. When anyone hears the word of the kingdom and does not understand it, the evil one comes and snatches away what has been sown in his heart. This is the one on whom seed was sown beside the road. The one on whom seed was sown on the rocky places, this is the man who hears the word and immediately receives it with joy; yet he has no firm root in himself, but is only temporary, and when affliction or persecution arises because of the word, immediately he falls away. And the one on whom seed was sown among the thorns, this is the man who hears the word, and the worry of the world and the deceitfulness of wealth choke the word, and it becomes unfruitful. And the one on whom seed was sown on the good soil, this is the man who hears the word and understands it; who indeed bears fruit and brings forth, some a hundred-fold, some sixty, and some thirty. (Matt. 13:18–23)

This explains why some people never grow: They fail to fireproof their lives. They start out following Jesus but fall by the wayside. The devil trips them up and they ruin their testimony. One minute you see them praising God, the next minute they are on the inactive list. The seed of the Word never took root, so when the fires come through pain or persecution, they blow it.

> *The only seeds that bear fruit are those sown in soil conducive to bearing fruit.*

Others never mature because they are caught up in the things of the world. Fame, fortune, power and pleasure dominate their thinking. They get caught up in materialism, thinking only of themselves and worrying about how to protect the stuff they have and get more stuff they don't need. When the fire comes, all they've lived for goes up in smoke.

In the movie *Fireproof,* Caleb is searching for the perfect new boat, led astray by greed and materialism. Meanwhile, his marriage continues to crumble.

Notice that in the parable seventy-five percent of the seeds bear no lasting fruit. Most of the seeds fall on soil that has not been cultivated. The only seeds that bear fruit are those sown in soil conducive to bearing fruit. If our hearts are cluttered and uncultivated, we will fail when the tests of life come.

When Trouble Strikes

When a forest fire sweeps along the mountainside, the giant sequoias are rarely destroyed. They take their stand. While other less hearty trees are destroyed by the raging fire, the sequoia has, over hundreds of years, developed multiple layers of bark in preparation for the fire drill.

Within the bark of the sequoia is a substance called tannin, which acts as a natural fire retardant to neutralize the burning embers that embed themselves in the tree. Does this remind you of the shield of faith that is able to quench the fiery darts the Enemy shoots at us?

Here's another interesting fact about the sequoia: The fire attacks the base, the foundation of the tree. Due to the incredible height of the sequoia, the crown of the tree remains above the flames and is only singed by heat and smoke.

But as the crown of the sequoia stretches constantly toward the light in an effort to bring life to every cell, its tremendous height invites more opposition. These proud trees bear scars from hundreds of lightning strikes as signs of their battle for survival.

Some of these lightning strikes cut deep and cause parts of the tree to become useless, yet it continues to live. Although in June and July in the High Sierras there are countless lightning strikes, no ordinary strike can kill a sequoia.

The tree will survive, heal and remain unshaken and stalwart. Even the most powerful strikes on the most vulnerable areas of the tree can rarely destroy it. But while these attacks are not fatal, they are still painful; it takes years to overcome the assault.

Many of us have been bruised, hurt and burned by life. The scars run deep. We're often blindsided by something that reminds us of that painful experience, but through the power of the Spirit we can learn to endure and be enabled to stand. Whether we have a fireproof life or one that crashes and burns depends on whether or not we equip ourselves for the battles to come.

Another Enemy well-known for its attacks on the sequoias waits for the opportune moment and only strikes when a fire has heated and softened the bark. The California horntailed wasp bores into the bark and feeds on the beneficial insects living there. The fire wasp, as it is commonly called, will then try to bore to the heart of the tree and deposit deadly larvae deep within the inner layers.

> *Many of us have been bruised, hurt and burned by life. The scars run deep.*

Do you know people who seem to be constantly going through a battle? They just can't get a break. Trouble seems to follow them around. As soon as they make it through one battle, another one begins to rage. Remember Job? Wave after wave of bad news came crashing in on him. He never knew why. Job was unaware of the invisible confrontation going on between the Lord and the devil.

When God was looking for righteous men to use as examples, he turned to Noah, Daniel and Job. In Ezekiel 14 we find these three mentioned for their righteousness. Obviously there was something in those men that stood the test of time. One stood for God during a flood. One stood for God in the lions' den amid a pagan nation. One stood for God in the midst of trial and tribulation.

> Some through the waters, some through the flood,
> Some through the fire, but all through the blood.

Like these three Old Testament giants, the sequoia is an example of what it takes to be someone God can brag about. Over time the sequoias drop their lower branches through wind, fire, lightning or by choice. They lay aside childish, youthful things unfit for a mature tree. Even the upper branches are thinned out until only a few of the strongest and most strategically placed are held in a dome-like crown in order to absorb the maximum amount of sun and rain. They know what is important for sustaining life and purpose. Today thousands of sermons have been preached and books have been written about the greatness of Noah, Daniel and Job. Their faithfulness has been a resting place for many who have wondered at times if serving God is worth it.

Noah, Daniel and Job took many hits. They were laughed at and criticized; Job was even told to curse God and die. They probably faced moments when they wondered if it was worth it, but they survived their times of testing. Job was blameless and upright and feared God. Although he lost so much that was precious to him, he never cursed God. Although he had three friends he could have done without, he waited for God to answer. It may be no small coincidence that the book of Job is followed by Psalm 1. Maybe, just maybe, Job was the inspiration for that psalm.

The great sequoias are not deformed by harsh weather; the strongest, most direct winds actually serve to strengthen the trees rather than weaken them. As believers, if we find our lives rooted in Christ, we can stand up to the winds of adversity no matter how strong they blow.

Each blast of wind creates tiny fractures in the bark of a sequoia which produce a more pliable and resilient tree, able to bend but not break. If you've lived long enough, you've lived through numerous storms and the testing fires that will enable you to be steadfast and immovable under pressure.

Standing Tall

Do you have the resolve and tenacity to live a fireproof life? The tests will come. Others will fail, and you may find yourself in a hard winter of discouragement. Someone may whisper in your ear that serving God is not worth it. Stand up. Stand strong. Stand tall. Don't quit. You've come too far to give up now.

When the sequoia is old—after being struck by lightning, attacked by fires, stung by wasps and weathered by thousands of snowstorms—it stands resolute above all others, distinctive and majestic in its beauty. The branches are eight to ten feet in diameter. The roots run in a network reaching more than two hundred feet in width.

The giant sequoia keeps its youth far longer than any of its neighbors. The silver firs are old in their second or third century, pines in their fourth or fifth, but the big tree growing beside them is still in the bloom of its youth, growing in every feature when the pines have gotten old. The sequoia does not attain prime size and beauty before 1,500 years or become old before 3,000 years. The longevity of this remarkable tree is more impressive than its size. Millennium after millennium, whatever the forces may deliver, sequoias triumph over tempest and fire and time, fruitful and beautiful, giving food and shelter to multitudes of small creatures dependent on their bounty.

The great prophet Isaiah gave us words to live by. They are words for the fireproof life, for the storms, the trials and the fires that will come our way. "Yet those who wait for the LORD will gain new strength; they will mount up with wings like eagles, they will run and not get tired, they will walk and not become weary" (Isa. 40:31).

If you are ready to wait on the Lord for that new strength to soar like an eagle, read on.

This giant of the forest reaches incredible heights as it stretches constantly toward the light in an effort to absorb the maximum amount of sun. The roots run in a network radiating out from the trunk as much as two hundred feet.

For the Lord knows the way of the righteous,
but the way of the wicked will perish.
(Ps. 1:6)

2

Fireproof Your Life Right Now

FOR A NUMBER of years I had the privilege of serving
with two other men on the board of the contemporary
Christian group 4Him. Along with our wives, we were asked
to give advice, counsel and accountability to one of the most
popular and successful groups of the 20th century. One year
at a Gospel Music Association panel discussion prior to the
Dove Awards, one member of the group summed up how
valuable the board was in his eyes: "If it weren't for the accountability board, we probably wouldn't be together right
now."

During those board meetings we learned to pray, to get
honest with one another, to hold each other accountable
and to grow together. This is what true Christian fellowship
is. If I want to fireproof my life, I must be open to constructive criticism, suggestions and insight from other believers.
If I'm not teachable, I'll lose my footing at some point on
my journey.

All of us know that relationships are tested, whether in a singing group, a marriage, a family or the workplace. How we respond to those tests can determine whether we are a success or a statistic.

I want my life to be a story of God's faithfulness and my obedience. I want to be someone my wife and kids can be proud of, as well as a pastor who leads his church properly. I don't want to be a casualty.

One of my favorite songs recorded by 4Him was entitled "A Man You Would Write About."

> *From the time time began*
> *   You always chose a man*
> *To lead the people safely by Your way*
> *   To be a voice and echo what You say*
>
> *Like David or Abraham*
> *   Your Word is full of such men*
> *And if the Bible had no closing page*
> *   And still was being written to this day*
>
> *I want to be a man that you would write about*
> *   A thousand years from now that they could read about*
> *Your servant of choice in whom You found favor*
> *   A man who heard Your voice*
>
> *Generations away it is my prayer*
> *   That they will look back and say,*
> *"Oh, to have that kind of faith and love.*
> *   What a solid man of God he was."* [1]

Success by God's Standards

Often when people are written of, it's about their failures and downfalls. We read of professional athletes getting caught using performance-enhancing drugs. We hear the sad tales of preachers who are lured into pornography or immorality. We learn that a couple in our Bible study is getting a divorce. The casualties are so common we are no longer shocked when people fall. In fact, we've come to expect it and accept it as normal.

A popular secular magazine in the 1990s did an article on the subject of success. The article, "The Best of the New Generation," dealt with successful people under the age of forty who were being used to impact and change America. They were recognized for things like taking risks, having initiative or being creative and persistent.

It is obvious to me now as I think back on the article that it was immersed in post-modern thought. Nothing was mentioned about morals, integrity, biblical values or character. Apparently success in our society doesn't involve the condition of the heart. But God sees things differently. God has a job description for a successful person that reveals the things He is looking for in an individual. In the Bible's description of success, there are characteristics to follow and observations to be noted.

The first psalm defines success in terms of character, not vocation. Success isn't about money; it's about lasting value. This psalm is the first song of the Jewish hymnal and gives us a vivid contrast between the righteous and the wicked, a pattern seen consistently through Scripture: saved and lost, blessed and cursed, wise and foolish.

The reason we don't have fireproof lives is because we believe there is middle ground. We have bought the lie that compromise is acceptable. If a person does not make the Word of God his guide, the way of God his aim and the will of God his one desire, he will always be susceptible to failure.

If, however, we want to live a blessed life that is pleasing to the Lord, there are specific things that must be part of our daily living. We must pay attention to what God says. If we desire to survive the fires of life, we need to know how to fireproof our motives.

People are looking for happiness and blessing. Unfortunately, they often look in the wrong places, causing them to get off track and ultimately fall. They stumble along the way because they look anywhere but to the Lord for peace, joy and happiness. We seal our fate by the choices we make. "Enter through the narrow gate; for the gate is wide and the way is broad that leads to destruction, and there are many who enter through it. For the gate is small and the way is narrow that leads to life, and there are few who find it" (Matt. 7:13–14).

Psalm 1 begins with a blessing and ends with a curse. It is a passionate declaration of the psalmist to seek the ways of God and a warning to avoid the ways of the wicked. It is an Old Testament reminder of Paul's words in First Corinthians: "Let him who thinks he stands take heed that he does not fall" (10:12).

Psalm 1:1

How blessed is the man who does not walk in the
    counsel of the wicked,
Nor stand in the path of sinners,
Nor sit in the seat of scoffers!

The writer begins by looking at life from a negative perspective. I know that's not popular in today's feel-good, me-centered American Christianity, but it's a good place to start. There is a negative side to godliness; there are things that a godly person can't do. This is not about legalism, it's about lordship. The spiritual side of our nature is completely opposed to the depraved side of our nature, and this battle will continue as long as we live. In our flesh dwells no good thing. We are wretched.

When my wife Terri and I first started in ministry, we worked with students and youth. During those fifteen years we were blessed to see God work in the lives of young people who wanted to go deeper with the Lord.

Three principles I learned from Dr. Jerry Vines became a key to my student ministry. Speaking on the three Hebrew children in the fiery furnace, he

> *The spiritual side of our nature is completely opposed to the depraved side of our nature, and this battle will continue as long as we live.*

made a statement I've never forgotten: "They wouldn't bow. They wouldn't bend. They wouldn't burn." If we're going to live fireproof lives, we would do well to remember those three principles.

First, they wouldn't bow to the culture. All around us believers, pastors and churches are caving in to the culture, allowing the world to influence the church instead of the church influencing the world. We are no longer salt and light, we're sugar and spice. We cannot allow our lives to be absorbed in stinking thinking. We have to renew our minds daily and die daily.

Second, they wouldn't bend to the whims of the times. Today's system is aggressively trying to make us politically correct. We can't cater to these demands and remain true to the gospel. There is nothing new under the sun. Sin is still sin, and the cross is still the cross. The flesh dies hard. The Enemy's tactics haven't changed much over the years. Whatever our Enemy and this world's system try to impose on us is, in essence, vanity.

Third, they wouldn't burn under the fires of pressure. They maintained their testimony while facing the flames of adversity. The goal of the evil one and those who follow him is to destroy your testimony and your witness. When black and white become dingy gray, the world feels better about itself. We must stand tall with our armor on. The fiery darts are coming.

You and I know what we are supposed to do—doing it is the key. Vance Havner said, "Most church members live so far below the standard, you'd have to backslide to be in fellowship. We are so subnormal that if we were to become normal, people would think we were abnormal."[2]

Those who think they can live a compromised life are in danger of failure. The Israelites grew weary of fighting the Canaanites and chose peaceful coexistence. It didn't work. There is no peaceful coexistence with evil. Apathy, compromise, loose values—playing with fire will ultimately get you burned. James said, "Submit therefore to God. Resist the Devil and he will flee from you" (4:7). But we often try to resist without submitting. You can't say "no" to the Devil without first saying "yes" to God.

When you see someone who calls himself a believer but is continually found walking and talking in the ways of the world, enjoying the company of the ungodly more than fellowship with the saints, you have to wonder when the fall is going to come.

Notice in the first verse of Psalm 1 the progressive nature of sin, the downward spiral toward a wasted life. There are three sets of triplets:

- **walk** in the **counsel** of the **wicked**
- **stand** in the **path** of **sinners**
- **sit** in the **seat** of **scoffers**

When the psalmist refers to our "walk" he is talking about how we make daily decisions based on our worldview. When he uses "stand" he's referring to our commitments to a particular way of life. The word "sit" is a reference to a settled attitude of the heart. It implies total identification. Godly people watch where they go and whom they listen to.

In a society that no longer views the laws of God as guidelines for lifestyle, politics or society in general, it is imperative for the godly to make right choices and stand strong.

If we desire to be holy and blameless people, we must oppose godless thinking and living. We cannot be found standing in the path of sinners. This refers to a deliberate violation of God's law. The Hebrew word "sinners" is a picture of someone who makes a loud noise, causes turmoil or provokes a disturbance. The godly person doesn't make trouble.

In a society that no longer views the laws of God as guidelines for lifestyle, politics or society in general, it is imperative for the godly to make right choices and stand strong. We have a powerful witness when we are unstained by the world. We can't be the people of God if we lack discernment and have more confidence in Oprah and Dr. Phil than in the Word of God. Any principle not based on God's standards will lead you down the path of scoffers.

If you listen to the counsel of the self-willed or imitate the conduct of the self-sufficient or seek the company of scoffers, you will ultimately fail. Listening to them will result in the development of ungodly principles. If you sit around with sarcastic mockers, you'll establish unholy partnerships.

No one becomes ungodly overnight, though. When you see someone falter in the family of faith, it's usually not a blowout. It's the result of a small leak in their soul, some area where they let their guard down or justified something inexcusable.

A characteristic of scoffers is to blame everyone but themselves for what is wrong in their lives. When confronted by the consequences of their actions they make excuses. They blame their environment, their heritage, their family, their peers, the computer or the system but never take personal responsibility.

The "wicked," or the ungodly, are those who live their lives without any thought of God. They have no point of reference in regard to the Lord. Just as 7Up® was called the "un-cola," with no cola in their product, the ungodly lack anything of God in their lives. But every day believers "ooh" and "ahh" over stars and celebrities whose lives are not worth imitating.

A wicked person is not just a mobster or a murderer or

an abortionist. A wicked person is anyone who does not have time for God in his or her life. Wicked people rule out God in their agenda and order of business. This should sound a warning bell to believers. If we rule out God by being unfaithful to the Scriptures, by not spending time with God in His Word and in prayer, wouldn't that also be considered "wicked" in the eyes of God?

One reason our lives end up in shambles is we've bought into the lies of the world. Such ideas as "Look out for #1," "I have a right to live the way I want," and "It's OK to bend the rules if you don't get caught" are worldly attitudes that can often appear very persuasive.

The writer of Psalm 1 doesn't fall for it, though. He questions and challenges the enlightenment of this present age. He sees people making dead-end choices and he sees the consequences that result. You cannot miss the downward spiral here. Those who end up blowing it begin by walking along, then at some point hesitating and standing around to listen. Then they decide to sit down and take in what they're hearing. It's a lifestyle choice, a decision to hang out with the wrong crowd. Once a person reaches that point, only repentance and removal can save them from tragic failure.

All of us know people who once walked with God who now care nothing for His ways. At one time they taught a Bible study class, but now they couldn't care less about the Word of God. They used to respect the things of God, but now they mock and scoff at those who are so "narrow-minded." What happened?

I grew up with a guy who was the greatest soul winner I've ever known. He loved Jesus and lived for Him as a college athlete and ministerial student. But something happened when he went off to seminary. He became an intellectual and started to question God's Word. He became too "wise" for the simple truths of Scripture. He received his doctorate but was ignorant in the ways of God and the schemes of the Devil. Today he is out of the ministry, divorced and teaching a humanistic worldview at a secular university. What a tragedy for the Kingdom.

If our lives are going to be fireproof, they have to bear witness that we are strangers and aliens in this world.

There is an interesting tone to Psalm 1, something you don't often hear in the church today. While the "health-and- wealth" crowd tells us to emphasize the positive, God begins by pointing out the negative. The blessed man is distinguished by the things he doesn't do, the places he refuses to go, the books he will not read, the movies and TV programs he will not watch, and the company he can't afford to keep. Paul reminded the Corinthians, "Do not be deceived: Bad company corrupts good morals" (1 Cor. 15:33).

Too often believers find themselves in the counsel of the wicked. It is wicked counsel to think I can live life on my terms and call myself a follower of Jesus Christ. In fact, living life on my terms not only sets me up to fail, but it is also really nothing more than practicing atheism with a religious facade.

If our lives are going to be fireproof, they have to bear witness that we are strangers and aliens in this world. This world is not our home; we're just passing through. What difference does it make if you are flying first class by the world's standards if you are on the wrong plane?

Psalm 1:2

But his delight is in the law of the LORD,
And in His law he meditates day and night.

While the first verse of Psalm 1 describes the negative, verse 2 presents the positive side of a blessed life. A person with a fireproof life delights in the Word of God. He meditates on it day and night. When the psalmist refers to the Law, he's not just referring to the Torah or the Ten Commandments, but to all of God's revelation.

The fireproof life is also characterized by an appropriation of the Word. Delight is expressed in meditation. Jeremiah 15:16 says, "Your words were found and I ate them, and Your words became for me a joy and the delight of my heart; for I have been called by Your name, O LORD God of hosts." Although I'm not a fan of formulas, I'm going to give you one here:

Love for the Lord + Love for His Law = A Lifestyle of Godliness

After surrendering his life to Christ, Caleb understands the importance of studying God's Word.

Psalm 1:3

He will be like a tree firmly planted by streams of water,
Which yields its fruit in its season,
And its leaf does not wither;
And in whatever he does, he prospers.

The evidence of a fireproof life is in a person's character. Don't miss this principle: The godly have learned in the hidden, inner parts of their lives to draw on the grace of God.

The metaphor of trees is common in the Bible—the godly are like trees. When you see a great sequoia you think of strength, steadfastness and stability. The tree planted by streams of water is symbolic of a life planted in Christ. In Christ we never worry about a dry season because the River of Life never runs dry. Jesus said, "If you are thirsty, come to Me!"

A tree does more than stand still. It produces oxygen, shade and sometimes fruit. Trees support life. They are a shelter in the storm. When I think of the sequoias I am reminded of what Paul said to the Corinthians: "Therefore, my beloved brethren, be steadfast, immovable, always abounding in the work of the Lord, knowing that your toil is not in vain in the Lord" (1 Cor. 15:58). To the Colossians he wrote, "If indeed you continue in the faith firmly established and steadfast, and not moved away from the hope of the gospel that you have heard, which was proclaimed in all creation under heaven" (Col. 1:23).

Fruit is the external evidence of an internal life. People who are rooted in Christ will produce the fruit of the Spirit. A fruitful tree doesn't just take up space; it produces something that is a benefit and blessing to others.

The psalmist continues, "its leaf does not wither." That refers to an exhibition of consistency and steadfastness. In the part of the country where I live, pine trees and evergreens abound. Evergreens are not seasonal; they are steadfast.

I'm not a nature person, but I do know that dry leaves are the result of dry roots. Often in the south the heat can be unbearable. If you don't have a sprinkler system, the trees easily wilt and the leaves wither. The leaf of the tree reflects the condition of the roots.

A fireproof life is a life that is blessed and will bless others. The phrase "in whatever he does, he prospers" in Psalm 1:3 does not refer to material possessions. Rather it refers to maturity. In spite of what the prosperity preachers say today, a man is not prosperous because he has cars, lands and money. You can have all that and not be blessed. In fact, many who have all the worldly possessions they could ever want are the most miserable people in the world. Nothing satisfies them.

We prosper as our soul prospers. True wealth is not found in the size of an estate or bank account, but in sound character and a commitment to laying up treasures in heaven.

The person who has determined to live a fireproof life may have nothing, yet possesses everything. Against that kind of person the Devil can make little headway. He might say, "Serve me and I'll give you whatever you want." The fireproof life responds, "You can't give me anything because I already have everything." The Devil may say, "I will take away what you have," but the believer replies, "You can't, because I don't have anything." Satan may say, "I can take your life," to which the Christian responds, "For me to live is Christ and to die is gain."

Psalm 1:4–6

This Psalm ends with a warning as a reminder of what happens to the ungodly:

The wicked are not so [firmly planted],
But are like chaff which the wind drives away.
Therefore the wicked will not stand in the judgment,
Nor sinners in the assembly of the righteous.
For the Lord knows the way of the righteous,
But the way of the wicked will perish.

"Not so"—in two words we see everything said about the believer is irrelevant to the unbeliever. Also it reminds us that this world's system will not stand when God sends the fires of judgment. Chaff lacks the sturdy stability of a firmly planted tree. When God begins to sift, chaff cannot stand. The future of the ungodly is doom and damnation. Chaff is worthless. It has no value and it is easily blown away.

Do you desire a fireproof life? Are you a person God would want to write about?

Do you desire a fireproof life? Are you a person God would want to write about? If by chance God were rewriting Hebrews 11, the Hall of Fame of the Faithful, would He even look your way?

When Paul was a prisoner to Nero, he was in the hands of the most cruel, vain, inhumane Caesar that had ever led the Roman Empire. Nero commanded all to bow to him, and was feared throughout the empire. In contrast, Paul was an obscure Jew who had come to Christ, known only in a few areas of the empire. He spent most of his life being beaten or in prison. Yet today we name our sons Paul and our dogs Nero.

What are some keys to fireproofing your life? Several years ago I had the privilege of attending a pastors' conference with the late Adrian Rogers from Bellevue Baptist Church in Memphis, Tennessee. In a session called "Keeping Pace," Dr. Rogers gave us a bonus: a list of declarations which he used to make sure his life was usable. I took notes as fast as I could and have kept them in my prayer notebook ever since. Like me, you may want to write this down so you can refer to it often.

Praise: I praise God that He has given Himself for me. I praise Him for something new every day. I praise Him for my salvation, redemption, the cross and the indwelling Holy Spirit.

Acceptance: I accept that He has given Himself to me. I accept who I am in Christ. (Just take a concordance and go through the passages in the New Testament where Paul refers to "in Christ" or "with Christ" or "through Christ." It will change the way you think. You'll develop Biblical self-esteem.)

Control: I place myself under the control of God so that He can live His life through me. I give myself to His lordship. I take up my cross. I die daily. It is not I, but Christ.

Expectation: I believe it's going to be a great day as I live my life with Him. It's going to be a day where I can be used by God. I make the choice to rejoice.

It takes twenty-one days to start a habit. How about trying to "keep pace" spiritually for the next twenty-one days? Start each day with these simple yet profound thoughts. Who knows, when the fire comes, you might be able to praise God, accept what's happening, surrender yourself and expect God to show you something great in the midst of the fire.

Remember how Psalm 1 ends: "The LORD knows the way of the righteous, but the way of the wicked will perish" (1:6).

Within the bark of the sequoia is a substance called tannin, which acts as a natural fire retardant to neutralize the burning embers that embed themselves in the tree—like the shield of faith that quenches the fiery darts of the enemy. A sequoia can live through many fires, but afterward the tree can smolder for six to twelve months.

... your faith, being more precious than gold which is perishable, even though tested by fire, may be found to result in praise and glory and honor at the revelation of Jesus Christ.
(1 Pet. 1:7)

3

Fireproof Your Faith

I GREW up in a typical Baptist church. We started at eleven o'clock sharp with the prelude and ended at twelve o'clock dull with the benediction. It seemed the pastor never expected God to do anything. No one expected anyone to respond to the invitation. The church, for most of my growing up years, was dull, dead and faithless.

Little of faith, discipleship or commitment was ever mentioned. I recall a lot of hot air but no wind of the Spirit.

Manley Beasley was the greatest man of faith I ever met. Two of his children served on our staff, and we often talked about their dad's faith. Manley's youngest son, Jonathan, once said to me, "The hardest thing about being dad's son is learning to develop your own faith. When dad was alive, we depended so much on his faith for us. Now that he's gone, we're having to learn what it means for us personally to walk by faith."

Manley had survived numerous (I'm not exaggerating) incurable diseases. He was as sure as dead more times than anyone can count. He wrote a fantastic workbook on faith that will take you places you've never been. Manley often asked people, "What are you trusting God for today?" Many Christians haven't trusted God for anything since trusting Him for salvation, which is why the saints burn out. They walk by sight, and not by faith.

Four times in Scripture we are told "the just shall live by faith." I came to Christ by faith, and I continue in Christ by faith.

We all want great faith. We just don't want to pay the price. When I saw the faith of Manley Beasley, I wanted it— but to be honest I didn't (and still don't) want to go through the fires he went through to get it.

What Faith Looks Like

Ron Dunn said, "All that believes is not faith, and much of what is being called faith today is not faith at all. Any day now someone is going to sue God for breaking a promise."[1] I would dare say, in light of much we hear today about faith, many are confused about what Biblical faith looks like. When you listen to the "health-and-wealth" crowd, faith would seem to mean a new car, on-the-spot healing, lots of money and the repentant return of prodigals. That's not reality. Faith is not a *carte blanche* to supernatural power.

The other extreme is the failure to believe God altogether. Four times in Scripture we are told "the just shall live by faith." I came to Christ by faith, and I continue in Christ by faith. But what is faith? How would we define it from a Biblical perspective?

Ron Dunn explained it this way:

"One, faith is an affirmation. It's our 'amen' to all God has revealed about Himself.

"Two, it is an act. We obey all God commands.

"Three, it is an attitude. It is believing that God is actively interested and involved in our daily existence. And it is this attitude of faith, this resting in Him, that God desires most."[2]

What do others say when they try to define faith?

- At the end of the day, faith means letting God be God. (John Blanchard)
- Faith is the capacity to trust God while not being able to make sense out of everything. (James Kok)
- Faith is the sight of the inward eye. (Alexander MacLaren)
- Faith is the power of putting self aside that God may work unhindered. (F. B. Meyer)
- Faith is reason at rest in God. (C. H. Spurgeon)
- Faith does not look at itself. It has no value save as it links us with God. (Vance Havner)
- Faith is not idle; it works while it waits. (Ron Dunn)[3]

Faith is not wishful thinking, presumption, a denial of reality, the power of positive thinking or positive confession. Faith, according to Hebrews, is "the assurance of things hoped for, the conviction of things not seen" (11:1). As you study the Scriptures you find faith tied to words like "knowing," "believing" and "obeying" the truth. If you don't believe that our God is trustworthy, you'll never be able to walk by faith. Psalm 9:10 says, "Those who know Your name will put their trust in You." The emphasis of the Bible is not on our subjective experiences but on the object of our faith—God Himself.

Mustard Seed Faith

We are to have faith in God and His Word. In my office I have a very small jar filled with mustard seeds. Although it

Faith is the starting point on the road to obedience. It is our foundation and sustaining strength in the storms of life.

is only an inch-and-a-half long and about a half-inch wide, it contains hundreds of mustard seeds. I bought the jar in Israel as a visible reminder of one of the great teachings of our Lord.

I've often looked at that little jar and wondered, *What could I do if I had faith the size of one of those tiny mustard seeds? What could my church do if we had just a few hundred people with mustard-seed faith?* The possibilities are limitless. The embarrassing reality is that most of us fail the tests of faith.

Faith is the starting point on the road to obedience. It is our foundation and sustaining strength in the storms of life. I don't really have faith if I'm not living according to what I say I believe about God and His Word. Too often we can talk a better game than we can live.

Think about just a few of those who were called to put their faith to the test. Remember, they obeyed God in spite of the circumstances or public opinion. They acted apart from rational explanations or physical evidence. They believed God because they knew that authority for faith is the revelation of God.

Noah, build an ark.

"Are You kidding, Lord? What's an ark?"

Abraham, set out for a city.

"What city? Aren't You going to give me a map?"

Abraham, you're going to have a child.

"At my age? Do You know how old my wife is?"

Joseph, I've got big plans for you.

"Lord, You're going to have to get me out of this prison first. I'm a forgotten man."

Israel, take the land.

"Are You crazy? We're grasshoppers and they're giants." (Remember the Bible records the failures of faith and its consequences as well as the stories of those who trusted God and took Him at His Word).

David, you are going to be the next king of Israel.

"How? If I don't keep running, King Saul is going to kill me!"

Elijah, pray down fire from heaven.

"Are You sure, Lord? It seems to me I'm outnumbered."

Job, trust Me with your loss and pain.

"Lord, nobody knows the trouble I've seen."

Isaiah, prophesy in My name.

"Lord, don't You know my friend the king just died? I'm grieving right now."

Jeremiah, buy the land.

"Lord, I'm no expert in real estate, but it seems to me that's not a very good deal."

Micah, tell them Messiah will come from Bethlehem.

"Lord, most folks can't even find Bethlehem on the map."

Peter, get out of the boat.

"And do what? Walk on water?"

When I think about faith, I am reminded of the situation that arose when Jesus talked about mustard-seed faith. Shortly after the Transfiguration, Jesus, Peter, James and John were coming down the mountain. The other disciples were with a man whose son was demonized. He had asked the other disciples to deliver the boy, but they could not.

After Jesus cast out the demon, "the disciples came to Jesus privately and said, 'Why could we not drive it out?' And He said to them, 'Because of the littleness of your faith; for truly I say to you, if you have faith the size of a mustard seed, you will say to this mountain, "Move from here to there," and it will move; and nothing will be impossible to you'" (Matt. 17:19–20).

Warren Wiersbe writes, "Faith as a grain of mustard seed suggests not only size (God will honor even a little faith), but also life and growth. Faith like a mustard seed is living faith that is nurtured and caused to grow. Faith must be cultivated so that it grows and does even greater exploits for God (1 Thess. 3:10, 2 Thess. 1:3). Had the nine disciples been praying, disciplining themselves, and meditating on the Word, they would have been able to cast out the demon and rescue the boy."[4]

If we want God's sustaining power in our lives during difficult times, we need to learn to flex our faith muscles. It's not the size but the object of our faith that matters. Mountain-moving faith is in the power of God. The use of the term "seed faith" by many televangelists (to mean "big faith produces big results") misrepresents the term.

Mustard-seed faith doesn't see the obstacles; it focuses on our God, who is greater than any obstacle we might face. I can acknowledge that a problem exists, but looking at life through the eyes of faith, the problem is never so big that God is not bigger still. It is His great power, not our great faith, that works in our times of testing. If our test seems mountainous, we need to get our eyes off the mountain and focus on the God who created heaven and earth.

The reality is, our faith is tested. We go through the fire. But we are called of God to step out in faith and believe Him.

Unbelief

In Psalm 78 we read these words: "They did not believe in God and did not trust in His salvation. . . . they still sinned and did not believe in His wonderful works" (78:22, 32).

How incredibly strange that God's people, who had seen the hand of God working so mightily on their behalf, would act in such a way. God delivered them. He met them at their point of need and fed their hunger. But as you read this psalm you quickly discover their lack of appreciation. In fact, they questioned whether God was capable of fulfilling His purpose in their lives. They believed God enough to leave Egypt, but they lacked the faith to step into the Promised Land.

Instead of walking by faith into all God had promised, they whined in the wilderness. And they died in the wilderness because of their unbelief. They had the Promised Land before them, but they chose to eat dust and bury the dead.

They reached a level of testing where they were unwilling to continue on with God. When we go through the fire storms of life, we have a choice: Do we believe God or do we quit? Will we pass or fail the fire inspection? Faith is a demonstration that the disciples of our Lord refuse to accept failure as final. We know God has the last word.

Far too often we know God's plan and we've read His Word, but we choose to make our own plans and figure out a fleshly "fire escape" just in case God doesn't come through. This is a sign of unbelief. We are self-deceived when we try to "help" God or when we think we can handle life's tests and trials on our own.

Faith must fix its attention on the power and promises of God alone. Our strengths are no help to God and our weaknesses no hindrance. Yet, we are slow to trust the Almighty. Rather than resting on His omnipotence, we struggle and wrestle with life in our own strength. What God wants is obedience and the yielding of our will to His.

Faith must fix its attention on the power and promises of God alone. Our strengths are no help to God and our weaknesses no hindrance.

A. B. Simpson wrote, "The larger the God we know, the larger will be our faith. The secret of power in our lives is to know God and expect great things from Him." If we want to see our faith grow, it has to be tested. God wanted to grow the children of Israel so He put them to a test. When was the last time you expected to find God in the fire? Faith doesn't make things easy, but it does make much possible.

Ron Dunn wrote, "If only a soul can believe in God . . . it can obtain anything that is in the heart of God to bestow." Notice he didn't say it can obtain anything it wants. He said it can obtain what's in the heart of God.

We are to walk by faith, not by sight. Abraham, as the years went by and the promise remained unfulfilled, looked at himself and his wife and said, "No way." The result of his lack of faith was called Ishmael. Rather than waiting on the promise, Abraham and Sarah decided to help God out. While

Abraham is the father of the faithful, he's also the father of a son who was the result of unbelief. As the testing wore on, Abraham became impatient with the Lord. He wasn't getting any younger, you know!

Although Abraham knew the plans and promises of God, he set out to make his own plans. You can read his story of unbelief in Genesis 16. Initially, after God renewed the promise in chapter 15, Abraham believed God. But as time went on, he became impatient. All he had to do was wait for God's timing, but he caved in to his flesh and conceived a child with Hagar. In Abraham's eyes he had planned and gotten what God had promised—a son. But there was a problem: It was not by faith but by the flesh. The unbelief of the father of the faithful caused many heartaches.

The same is true with us. We read the promises, listen to the sermons, hear testimonies of other people's faith in God; but then try to strike out on our own. There's a price to pay for trying to do God's will our own way. Peter reminded us that God has given us "precious and magnificent promises" (2 Pet. 1:4). We can't force the promises; we can only trust God to fulfill them in His own time and way.

Passing the Faith Test

Abraham learned from his mistake; he never wavered in his faith again. The New Testament presents Abraham as the ultimate illustration of the faith life. Paul told the Romans, "Abraham believed God, and it was credited to him as righteousness" (4:3). Everything Abraham needed and everything God demanded of him was obtained by faith.

Frank A. Clark said, "A fellow shouldn't abandon his faith when it weakens, any more than he would throw away a suit because it needs pressing." There may be a time when it's hard to find God in your fire, but you can always trust He is there.

When we go through a trial, our faith is being tested. We can talk about faith all we want, but until our faith is tested we don't know the validity or the depth of our faith. Until we've thrown ourselves on God's mercy and seen God in the storm, we haven't looked with the eyes of faith. "Our faith is really and truly tested," wrote John Calvin, "only when we are brought into very severe conflicts, and when even hell itself seems opened to swallow us up."

All of us will be tested. All of us will be given a choice to trust our flesh or trust the Father. If you want a fireproof faith, you need to learn some principles from Abraham. After Abraham learned his lesson with Ishmael, God fulfilled His promise with Isaac. Abraham could take some credit for Ishmael, but not for Isaac. What can we learn from this?

1) **A fireproof faith has confidence in God.** Abraham believed God. The object of faith determines its validity. Abraham no longer trusted in himself, but learned to trust the God who makes the impossible possible—the God of creation who makes something out of nothing, the God of the resurrection who makes life out of death.

When you are going through a test of your faith, you have two options: You can fall into the trap of saying, "It's no use; I give up. I've prayed and nothing is happening." Or, you can say, "My God is faithful and true. He has never failed to honor His Word. Nothing is impossible with Him." You can choose to cooperate with the omnipotent God of glory. It was said of Abraham, "In hope against hope, he believed" (Romans 4:18). When there was no way, Abraham said, "God has a way." He believed that he might become all God had called him to be.

2) A fireproof faith does not ignore or deny problems. Faith is not living in denial. God made a promise that led Abraham to trust God's word instead of getting caught up in the difficulties. God specializes in problem situations. If He can handle the sin problem, He can handle the saint's problems.

3) A fireproof faith is expressed through confidence in the Word of God. Abraham examined the situation and determined that in spite of his age, in spite of the fact he had failed with Hagar and Ishmael, God could be trusted. The Bible says, "The just shall live by faith." The Hebrew word for "faith" means firmness or certainty.

4) A fireproof faith must become a way of life. We don't go through just one fire in the Christian life. You are either in the midst of a fire, coming out of one or headed for one. A fireproof faith is not insurance to escape hell; it's the capacity to live through hell while on earth. Abraham did not waver in unbelief. He was more sure of what God said than what his body was telling him as the years passed.

Faith is the key to the Christian life. Without it we can't please God. Anything we do apart from faith is sin. Jim Cymbala said, "What is faith? It is total dependence upon God that becomes supernatural in its working."

If I want to fireproof my life, I've got to learn what it means to walk by faith. There is no such thing as a life that can avoid the fires, trials and storms of life. There is, however, a life that overcomes. It is the life of faith.

Another enemy of the sequoias is the fire wasp, which attacks when a fire has heated and softened the bark. It bores into the bark and feeds on the beneficial insects living there. It will then try to bore to the heart of the tree and deposit deadly larvae deep within the inner layers. A healthy tree, however, is resistant to these pests.

And the peace of God, which surpasses all comprehension, will guard your hearts and your minds in Christ Jesus. (Phil. 4:7)

4

Fireproof Your Heart and Mind

A FIREPROOF LIFE is not a perfect life. If we think it's impossible for us to fail, we deceive ourselves. Remember what Paul said: "Let him who thinks he stands take heed that he does not fall" (1 Cor. 10:12). All of us know someone who didn't follow that admonition. The alarms were going off, but they didn't heed the warning. One tragic decision can lead to a fallen saint and a tarnished testimony. This is what happens when people do not take seriously the call to put on their armor and stay on their knees.

Some of us don't mature in our character because one part of us frustrates the rest. Our life is stalled in an internal debate. We set out to be all God wants us to be, but the inner battle rages and the mind is filled with contradictions. We give our old nature an audience by arguing with self, rather than doing what we know is right.

In the 1920s and '30s Vance Havner wrote a weekly column for *The Charlotte Observer*. In one article entitled "The Positive Life" the wise prophet wrote,

Every man has in him positive and negative elements. High thoughts, clean ideals, noble purposes, everything that elevates the tone of life and strengthens its moral fiber is positive. But low and dirty thinking, perverse inclinations, unworthy desires and everything that lowers the moral stamina, weakens the soul's morale, dulls the finer sensibilities and makes the spiritual less real is negative.

What to do with this mixed-up Inside Congress is our problem. If we make a debating society of our inner lives, we get nowhere and our time is frittered away in internal strife. The only way out is to live positively. Decide upon the highest and worthiest course of action, gather all the positive elements behind it and refuse to give the dissenters the floor.

Any man can tell which are the positives and negatives in his life. Let him give all his time to be positive and the opposition will die from neglect. Let him cultivate wholesome and constructive thinking, helpful friends, good books, uplifting tastes and pursuits and do only those things that build him up. The negative will pop up all along—we cannot help that—but we can refuse to accept, harbor and encourage it.

Particularly in our thought life do we need to discriminate. Negative thoughts are the germs of the spiritual life that infect us with poisons that undermine our integrity and destroy soul-health. Just as in the physical world, some constitutions can throw off these microbes better than others, but none of us can afford to tolerate them for the sturdiest will eventually give way if no action is taken.

All forms of fear, doubt, worry, all morbid, neurotic, unwholesome and vulgar tendencies, all moods, trials and whims that endanger our spiritual vitality must be shunned. When they appear, meet and counteract them with a positive. That is overcoming evil with good.

Do not linger with your inside parliament. Vote for the best you know and start doing right to carry the measure through. Hear only affirmative voices and the negative will die or line up with you. If you don't, the worst in you will veto the best. The Bible preacher had this in mind when he said, "Whatever things are true, honest, just, pure, lovely, of good report, think on these things."

Wise counsel from a wise man. There is much wisdom in the Bible on how to fireproof your mind and heart. Obviously it is centered on the truth of loving God with all your heart, soul, mind and strength.

Guard Your Heart

One reason I know the Bible is true is because its standards are high and holy. At the same time, God never tries to gloss over the failures of the heroes of faith. We see them realistically, warts and all. However, that doesn't allow us to make excuses. The examples of their unguarded moments are warnings to us.

When Alexander the Great was at the height of his power, he called in a famous artist to paint his portrait. The painting depicts Alexander with his head in his hands, as if he were thinking. Historians tell us otherwise. Alexander had a horrible scar on one cheek and was so ashamed that he hid the scar as he posed for the portrait.

The Holy Spirit does not hide the scars of the saints. He left them in the Word for our teaching, reproof, correction and training in righteousness.

"Now these things happened as examples for us, so that we would not crave evil things . . . they were written for our instruction" (1 Cor. 10:6, 11). Paul reminded the believers in Corinth, and us, that just because we have strong faith doesn't mean we are immune from fiery darts or our own flesh. Paul used Israel as an example to believers, lest we fall into the same traps.

Paul exhorted the Corinthians to live lives of self-discipline. Life is a battle with the world, the flesh and the Devil. We face persecution and temptation that can burn us if we aren't on guard. If our lives are going to stand up to the fire, we can't live as we please.

The Israelites experienced a powerful deliverance from Egypt, but it didn't take them long to forget. Look at their advantages: They had a godly leader in Moses, they saw great miracles and they had guidance from a great God. God brought them out of Egypt through the Red Sea, but they still turned away. They doubted and complained and, as a result, most of them never made it to the Promised Land.

Life is a battle with the world, the flesh and the devil. If our lives are going to stand up to the fire, we can't live as we please.

The Israelites were set free, but areas of their lives were unguarded. They did not guard their hearts, and their testimonies were burned by idolatry, sexual immorality, testing God and complaining. In each situation the consequences were death. When we fail to learn from their bad examples, we can make the same mistakes.

The reason we need to fireproof our lives is we are all idolaters at heart. Paul identified coveting as idolatry (see Col. 3:5). We make fame, fortune, power and possessions our gods. We can even worship our ministries and church positions. Sometimes we love others more than we love God, but seeking pleasure or delight in anything other than God is idolatry.

According to the *Evangelical Dictionary of Biblical Theology*,

> The testimony of Scripture is that God alone is worthy of worship. Active acknowledgment of idols by prostration, sacrifice, or other means of exaltation is not only a misdirection of allegiance; it robs God of the glory and honor that is rightfully his (Isa. 42:8). . . . The sense of Scripture was to destroy idolatry or be destroyed by it. Since idolatry presented an alternative world view the pressure to worship idols was felt in all aspects of life. Social idolatry became a family affair, involving cities, towns, clans, and tribes.[1]

Idolatry is a heart issue. In the New Testament it is associated with pride, self-centeredness, greed and gluttony. We can't read the Scriptures without seeing repeated warnings regarding idols. Idolatry is contrary to a Christian worldview. It is an attempt to offer an explanation for life apart from God's sovereignty.

Idolatry is also a head issue. When we begin to covet or love something other than God in the heart, the mind goes places it should not go and leads to dangerous choices. We take risks we can't afford.

There are three people in you today: the person you are, the person you could be for God and the person you could become if you let Satan get a foothold in your life. God sees the heart, and He knows our mind. We can lie to our friends and even try to lie to ourselves. But deep down inside we know when we are leaving a door open for the Enemy. "For who among men knows the thoughts of a man except the spirit of the man which is in him?" (1 Cor. 2:11).

In the movie *Fireproof*, Caleb Holt struggles with pornography. In one scene his wife Catherine walks in and asks him, "Did you clear your history?" referring to erasing the history on his computer to hide the websites he's been viewing. He tries to play dumb, but in reality his mind and heart are being lured into Internet porn. It affects his thoughts, his affection for his wife and his ability to understand what true love is all about. When confronted, he immediately becomes defensive. Only when he surrenders his life to Christ does he deal with the computer in a pointed (and humorous) way.

Tempers flare as Caleb and Catherine get into a heated argument about Caleb's pornography addiction.

I've heard it said that no one becomes involved in adultery, sexual abuse or homosexuality who has not first been affected by pornography. At one time you had to go to the store and buy a magazine, but now obscenity is everywhere. In fact, some studies suggest that the Internet is driven by pornographic sites. In the privacy of our homes, the Enemy uses the seclusion to seduce us to seek worldly pleasure. He entices us to feed the flesh with the simple click of a mouse.

Maybe that's why James said, "Submit therefore to God. Resist the Devil and he will flee from you" (James 4:7). Aren't we all guilty of trying to resist without submitting? Unfaithfulness begins in the mind before it is ever consummated in a cheap hotel. Sin is birthed, takes root and ultimately bursts forth to destroy our lives.

When I was a youth minister, I had two rules for youth camp:

1. Be where you are supposed to be, when you are supposed to be there, doing what you are supposed to be doing.
2. When in doubt, don't.

I told the kids if they would follow those rules, they would never get in trouble. Those same rules apply to us when it comes to fireproofong our hearts and minds.

Reaping the Consequences

The example of Israel is obvious. Paul uses it like a hammer to drive a pin into the inflated balloon of pride. Israel didn't do what they were told. When Moses was on the mountain meeting with God, they were in the valley dancing in the sand. Because Israel did not obey, they forfeited their right to the Promised Land for forty years. That's quite a price to pay for doing things their own way. They thought they knew better than God, so their hearts turned to worship a golden calf. They were overcome with fear of the giants in the land, and they turned away from taking God's promised inheritance. At every turn the Israelites are examples of how not to live the life of faith. They were tested and they failed.

Another example is David. With a single glance David began a downward spiral that almost destroyed him. One glance led to an act of adultery and then to a murder plot. He spent a year trying to cover up what he had done, but it ate away at his body and soul.

David was at the peak of his power and influence when he fell. At the time when kings were supposed to be going to war, David stayed in Jerusalem. The Bible says that "when evening came David arose from his bed" (2 Sam. 11:2). He was being lazy and it led to lust. If he had been where he was supposed to be, when he was supposed to be there, doing what he was supposed to be doing, he wouldn't have fallen into the trap set for him.

Lazy moments need to be feared more than hard labor. One misstep when you aren't spiritually sharp can ruin a reputation for a lifetime. An idle brain is the Devil's workshop. Thomas Brooks wrote, "Idleness is the very source of sin." The great prayer warrior E. M. Bounds said, "Our laziness after God is our crying sin. . . . No man gets God who does not follow hard after him." David grew lazy. He was probably middle-aged around this time. He had survived Saul's persecution and many other battles and had established his kingdom. Maybe he just decided to take a break, to chill out. After all, he had "earned" it.

> *Our idle days can become Satan's busiest days. It seems the enemy is always looking for an opportunity to work the most when we want to do the least.*

Our idle days can become Satan's busiest days. It seems the Enemy is always looking for an opportunity to work the most when we want to do the least. Richard Baxter said, "Laziness breeds a love of amusement."

One reason people are crashing and burning today is we are amusing ourselves to death. We want entertainment rather than enlightenment. We look for the latest gadgets instead of a deeper walk with God. When we pursue other things, God will eventually be shut out.

From his roof David saw Bathsheba bathing. Maybe he couldn't have avoided the first glance, but the stare was inexcusable. Our minds are like an airport runway—we can choose what we allow to land there. David's look turned to lust. He was careless with his thoughts, and it resulted in a carnal act. If you read the chapter (2 Samuel 11) you'll discover the progression. "He saw and sought," "He sent and inquired," "He took her and lay with her." Job said, "I have made a covenant with my eyes. How then could I gaze at a virgin" (Job 31:1)—or pornography or another woman?

David's sin was not merely an isolated act of adultery. His lustful actions led to a pregnancy, which ultimately led David to murder. Adultery was the hot-blooded sin; murder was cold-blooded. On the downward spiral of an unguarded heart and mind, David plotted the death of a trusted and loyal soldier. One of the Devil's lies is that we'll be satisfied if we fulfill a passion or appetite in a biblically inconsistent way. The very opposite is true: The more we feed the passion inappropriately, the more it grows and can't be fulfilled.

We know the effects of David's sin when we read his words in Psalm 32: "When I kept silent about my sin, my body wasted away through my groaning all day long. For

day and night Your hand was heavy upon me; my vitality
was drained away as with the fever heat of summer. Selah"
(32:3–4). After almost a year, David was finally honest with
himself and with God about his sin. No more cover-ups.
His carnal decision had hurt his family and tormented his
mind and body.

Note that David ends Psalm 32:4 with the word "Selah,"
which means, "to pause and think about it." We are told to
meditate on what's been said. Maybe Solomon had his own
father in mind when he wrote Proverbs 28:13, "He who con-
ceals his transgressions will not prosper, but he who con-
fesses and forsakes them will find compassion."

When God saved us, He didn't remove our capacity to
sin. He did put His Spirit within us to convict us of sin.
Falling down in a pool of water won't cause you to drown,
but lying face down in it will. David felt the heavy hand of
God on his life and finally surrendered to God in humility
and brokenness.

People who make no effort to fireproof their minds and
hearts end up doing one of three things:

They *rationalize*. They buy the lie of this world's system
and refuse to call sin what it is. They refuse to agree with
God.

They *get busy* and try to ignore the problem, wearing a
mask and becoming hypocrites. But busyness can't cover up
a barren life.

They *compare their sin* to someone else's. They say, "I
may have a problem, but I know people who are worse than
I am." Making excuses and pointing fingers will only lead
you down a path where your testimony will go up in smoke.
If we put off repenting another day, we have one more day

to repent of and one less day to repent in.

We need to be quick to respond to the convicting power and prompting of the Holy Spirit. Sometimes He will use the Word; sometimes He will use the loving rebuke of a brother or sister in Christ, like Nathan with David. Rather than playing games, we need to be quick to confess.

The Christ Life: Our Strength

The key to what people see of our lives is the inner life they don't see. "Set your mind on the things above, not on the things that are on earth. For you have died and your life is hidden with Christ in God" (Col. 3:2–3). Simply put, Christ's life was hidden in God. Our lives can be identified with His and share the same hiding place.

I doubt if anyone reading these pages hasn't longed for a life this world could not touch, worry, harass, damage or destroy. We desire to move through all the traps of trouble without fear or harm.

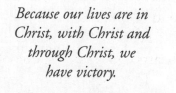

Because our lives are in Christ, with Christ and through Christ, we have victory.

Who wouldn't want an untouchable life, one beyond the reach of the fiery darts of the Enemy?

Jesus alone lived that kind of life. He moved through an antagonistic world and faced hostility, but it never moved Him. How did He do it? He had identified Himself with God the Father. You can't kill life. You can tear up the form it assumes, crucify the body it uses, but life itself can't be touched.

Incorporating Christ as our life sounds mystical. It is, in fact, very practical and possible. Our life can be hidden with Christ in God. Christ makes the thought a reality because He first lived that life for us. The last Adam empowers us to live as the first Adam never could. Because our lives are in Christ, with Christ and through Christ, we have victory.

Most believers who get burned have failed to understand basic truths about our life in Christ. Allowing our minds to drift from heavenly realities produces spiritually bankrupt lives. In his letter to the Romans, Paul wrote,

> Even so consider yourselves to be dead to sin, but alive to God in Christ Jesus. Therefore do not let sin reign in your mortal body that you should obey its lusts, and do not go on presenting the members of your body to sin as instruments of unrighteousness; but present yourselves to God as those alive from the dead, and your members as instruments of righteousness to God. For sin shall not be master over you, for you are not under law, but under grace. What then? Shall we sin because we are not under law but under grace? May it never be! (Rom. 6:11–15)

In Colossians 3 Paul uses the phrases "with Christ" and "with Him" to show us the sufficiency of our Savior. We must fill our minds with the Word of God and our hearts with this love, or we will fail to pursue the fullness of Christ. Paul tells us to "set" our minds, or think thoroughly about this. This is to be our inner disposition. J.B. Lightfoot paraphrases Paul's words with the following: "You must not only seek heaven, you must also think heaven."[2]

We have died. It happened the moment we were saved. The penalty and price of sin has been paid by our Defender, who lives within us. And that Presence within us is greater than he that is in the world. We are still aware of the presence and power of sin, but no longer condemned or controlled by it. We are hidden with Christ in God and are now "partakers of the divine nature" (2 Pet. 1:4).

Warren Wiersbe further expounds on our death with Christ: "The fullest explanation of this wonderful truth is found in Romans 6–8. Christ not only died for us (substitution), but we died with Him (identification). Christ not only died for sin, bearing its penalty; but He died unto sin, breaking its power. We are dead and alive at the same time—dead to sin and alive in Christ."[3]

The possibility can be reality. The hidden life makes it possible for the revealed life to be victorious. My life is fireproof when I understand that the world cannot reach my hidden, true source for living because God is my life.

We can be harassed, though. The fiery darts will come. But if we are hidden with Christ in God, we are overcomers through Christ our Lord. Dr. A.T. Robertson wrote, "So here we are in Christ who is in God, and no burglar, not even Satan himself, can separate us from the love of God in Christ Jesus."[4]

Romans 8 holds a beautiful reminder to us that our lives are fireproof in Christ:

> If God is for us, who is against us? He who did not spare His own Son, but delivered Him over for us all, how will He not also with Him freely give us all things? Who will bring a charge against God's elect? God is the one who justifies; who

is the one who condemns? Christ Jesus is He who died, yes, rather who was raised, who is at the right hand of God, who also intercedes for us. Who will separate us from the love of Christ?" (8:31–35)

In his commentary on Colossians, Warren Wiersbe writes,

> Someone has said, "Life is what you are alive to." A child may come alive when you talk about a baseball game or an ice-cream cone. A teenager may come alive when you mention cars or dates. Paul wrote, "For to me to live is Christ." Christ was Paul's life and he was alive to anything that related to Christ. So should it be with every believer.[5]

Let's identify some application points. The questions below serve as a guide for you as you get alone with the Lord and align your heart and mind with His.[6]

- Am I pure in heart? Are my motives pure? Have I laid down allegiances and affections I have cherished more than Jesus? Do I have single-minded devotion to Jesus Christ? (Matt. 5:8, 2 Cor. 11:3)
- Is my righteousness merely external, like that of the Pharisees, or does it come from my heart? (Matt. 5:20, 22:36–38)
- Do I have anything that is a master to me besides the Lord Jesus Christ? Am I holding on to anything that is causing me to treat Christ lightly or give Him less than His rightful place? (Matt. 6:24)
- Am I consistently in a position to hear the Word of God? Am I listening intently to God's voice to me, or am I merely paying casual attention? (Matt. 7:24)

- Am I actively and immediately obeying God as He speaks to my heart through His Word? (Matt. 7:24–27)

When a fire sweeps along the mountainside, the giant sequoias take their stand. The fire attacks the base of the tree, but due to its incredible height the crown of the tree remains above the flames and is merely singed by the heat. Other less hearty trees are destroyed by the raging flames, but the sequoia withstands its trial by fire with multiple layers of bark.

Submit therefore to God. Resist the
devil and he will flee from you.
(James 4:7)

5

Fireproof Your Convictions

ONE KEY to having a fireproof life is knowing how to survive the onslaught of Satan. Attacks will come because we are in a battle. Hardly a day goes by without hearing of some believer who has stumbled and fallen. When our lives start running at such a frantic pace that we run ahead of our character development, we quickly find ourselves in a danger zone. Living in the fast lane can make compromise look appealing.

In a survey by *Discipleship Journal* some years ago, readers were asked to list their strongest temptations. In order of priority, the "top ten" were:

- Materialism
  - Pride
    - Self-Centeredness
      - Laziness
        - Anger/Bitterness (tie)
          - Sexual Lust
            - Envy
              - Gluttony
                - Lying

Of those surveyed, 81% said they were more likely to yield to temptation when they neglected their time alone with God; 57% said they were more likely to yield when physically tired.[1]

We all face these temptations. At times I've let anger get a foothold. I've been in situations where I was wronged and could have easily allowed bitterness to take root in my life.

Some days I've been lazy in my pursuit of God. I've been jealous of another pastor and envied his position or his church. I have faced the temptation to lust. Jesus was so clear on the subject of lust and mental adultery that no man can claim to be exempt.

Materialism has tempted me. I've wanted something I didn't need to the point of being willing to go in debt to get it. After all, we have to keep up with the Joneses. The problem is, the Joneses are trying to keep up with us, and they just refinanced.

Even cheesecake has been so appealing to me that I couldn't resist, though the advice of my doctor was to push back from the table.

When confronted with these enticements, who hasn't been tempted to lie? We lie to cover our tracks. We lie to impress people. We lie to our spouses. When we sing songs in church that are not true of our lives, or say we believe the Word but don't do what it says, again, we lie.

I have a pastor friend whose father, also a pastor, fell into adultery. He said to his son, "Sundays are the hardest days of my life. I was born to preach and now I can't. I blew it because I cared about my flesh more than my faith."

Another friend, Dr. John Bisagno, the retired pastor of

First Baptist Church of Houston, has written in his Bible the names of over twenty "up and coming" young preachers who were in college with him.

By the time John was in his fifties, only three names were left on the list. All the rest had floundered, forsaken the ministry and taken a different path. They had neglected to guard their convictions.

> *The biggest problem we face is not knowing what is right, but being willing to do what is right.*

Temptation's Realities

Temptation is an invitation to do the wrong thing or even the right thing in the wrong way. Sin is the willingness to act on temptation. The biggest problem we face is not *knowing* what is right, but *being willing* to do what is right. Most of us have preset convictions on a variety of subjects. But how do we fireproof those convictions so they'll stand up under the weight of temptation?

Matthew's Gospel records the account of Jesus' own dealings with temptation.

Then Jesus was led up by the Spirit into the wilderness to be tempted by the Devil. And after He had fasted forty days and forty nights, He then became hungry. And the tempter came and said to Him, "If You are the Son of God, command that these stones become bread." But He answered and said, "It is written, 'Man shall not live on bread alone, but on every word that proceeds out of the mouth of God.'" Then the Devil took Him into the holy city and had Him stand on the pinnacle of the temple, and said to Him, "If

You are the Son of God, throw Yourself down; for it is written, 'He will command His angels concerning You'; and 'On their hands they will bear You up, so that You will not strike Your foot against a stone.'" Jesus said to him, "On the other hand, it is written, 'You shall not put the LORD your God to the test.'" Again, the Devil took Him to a very high mountain and showed Him all the kingdoms of the world and their glory; and he said to Him, "All these things I will give You, if You fall down and worship me." Then Jesus said to him, "Go, Satan! For it is written, 'You shall worship the LORD your God, and serve Him only.'" Then the Devil left Him; and behold, angels came and began to minister to Him. (Matt. 4:1–11)

First, let's establish some facts about temptation.

Temptation exists because we have a tempter. He's not a medieval character dressed in red with a pitchfork. He is the Prince of Darkness, the Accuser of the Brethren, and he is in rebellion against God.

Temptation is real and inevitable—you will be tempted—but it's not sin. If Lucifer tempted the sinless Son of God, then he is going to come after you—and you don't have to feel guilty about it!

Temptation often comes when we least expect it. Adam and Eve fell in the garden. Abraham shrank back on his walk of faith when he lied to Pharaoh. Elijah caved into discouragement and fear right after his victory on Mt. Carmel.

Temptation can come in the area of your strength. Your strengths can become your weakness. Remember, your talents and abilities are no help to God in empowering you to resist the Devil.

Temptation is allowed by God. The Spirit compelled Jesus to go out to the wilderness. The reality is this: Until your faith has been tested it hasn't been proven.

Temptation never stops. "When the Devil had finished every temptation, he left Him until an opportune time" (Luke 4:13). The Devil wasn't through trying, but he had exhausted his options at that point. Satan retreats in order to regroup.

Jesus was "led up by the Spirit into the wilderness." To the Jews of the first century the wilderness had both a good and a bad reputation. The bad reputation was that the wilderness was associated with demons (see, for example, Luke 11:24). The good reputation was that the wilderness was a place of spiritual retreat—a place where Moses, Abraham and the prophets went to escape the world's pressures and meet God in intimate fellowship. In the wilderness you're either going to meet God in a significant way or be overpowered by the Devil and give up.

In the wilderness of temptation there is both the possibility of strengthening and the potential for seduction. James gives us the order, "Submit therefore to God. Resist the Devil and he will flee from you" (4:7). We can't resist if we don't first submit.

Though temptation may take many subtle forms, Satan has three predictable methods of attack, which John summarized as "the lust of the flesh, the lust of the eyes and the boastful pride of life" (1 John 2:16). These are the same tactics he used in the Garden of Eden, and they have proven successful for centuries. (The Devil may be crafty, but he's not very creative!)

The Lust of the Flesh

First, Satan appeals to our flesh:

> And the woman said to the serpent, "From the fruit of the trees of the garden we may eat; but from the fruit of the tree which is in the middle of the garden, God has said, 'You shall not eat from it or touch it, lest you die.'" And the serpent said to the woman, "You surely shall not die! For God knows that in the day you eat from it your eyes will be opened, and you will be like God, knowing good and evil." (Gen. 3:2–5)

Satan lured Eve into sin by saying, "You have a right to be happy. You deserve more than you are getting. Since God made you like this, there's nothing wrong with satisfying your desires." To Jesus he said, "If you are the Son of God, and since you've been without food for forty days, why not tell these stones to become bread?" Think about it—if Moses could speak to a rock and see water come forth, surely the Son of God could turn stones to bread. Satan whispers, "You've got the desire, the need and the ability. Go ahead and satisfy the longings of your flesh."

When Satan made a demand on the deity of Christ, Christ responded as a man. "Man shall not live by bread alone." Jesus didn't overcome the appeal to His flesh on the basis of His deity, but on the basis of His humanity. He never used His power for His own benefit. He submitted Himself to the Word of God, not to the rumbling in His stomach.

Satan entices us to give in to our cravings and let our physical appetites dictate how we live. The key was not in

Jesus quoting Scripture. You can quote Scripture while eating your fifth jelly doughnut. The key is submitting your human desires to the authority of Scripture.

The Devil has a shallow view of man. He wants us to live on a shallow level. He tempts us to live according to our five senses. He knows that if you think life is to be found in living it up, you'll do everything in your power to please your flesh. But if you believe God's Word and know Christ as your sufficiency, you'll be able to stand on the authority of His Word, just as Jesus did.

> *The key is not in quoting Scripture. The key is submitting your human desires to the authority of Scripture.*

While the children of Israel were in the wilderness, God miraculously spared them by providing manna from heaven. "He humbled you and let you be hungry, and fed you with manna which you did not know, nor did your fathers know, that He might make you understand that man does not live by bread alone, but man lives by everything that proceeds out of the mouth of the LORD" (Deut. 8:3). Unfortunately they became ungrateful, murmuring and criticizing. Chuck Swindoll points out that when everything seems to be going well, you can expect surprise attacks from the Enemy.

> We get our theological ducks in a row, we make sure our eternal destination is sealed in a fireproof safe, we surround ourselves with a predictable schedule that protects us from contamination with the lost world, and then, like a 600-pound grizzly, we settle down for a long winter's snooze.
>
> Our hope? Do not disturb 'til the Rapture. And we're content to spend the balance of our lives as unconcerned

and uninvolved in our world as a silverfish crawling over a pile of discarded *Time* magazines.

Only one problem. The battle continues to rage, no matter what the season. From spring to summer. In relaxed autumn and icy winter. Whether we choose to believe it or not.

It is so easy to forget that our adversary, like our Advocate, neither slumbers nor sleeps. With relentless, unslacking energy . . . as sure as this morning's dawn, he's on the prowl, "seeking someone to devour" (1 Peter 5:8).

He's been at it for centuries. By means of a brilliant strategy, an insidious scheme, he takes advantage of our mental dullness. Surprise attacks are his specialty.

Small wonder Jesus kept urging His followers to "be on the alert," to "watch," to "resist," to keep a clean crop, free of stuff that "chokes the word, making it unfruitful."

Why? Because you never know when you are in the crosshairs of the scope of the Enemy's high-powered rifle. It could be today that you will be the target. When you least expect it . . . in the lazy days of summer, in the cool days of autumn, in the fog of false security, under the frost of a laid-back lifestyle.

He's looking for you. He's primed and ready to fire. And he doesn't wait for hunting season. In fact, as far as Satan is concerned, it's always open season on Christians.

Are you alert to the danger?[2]

The Lust of the Eyes

Satan's second method of attack is by appealing to our eyes:

And he led Him up and showed Him all the kingdoms of the world in a moment of time. And the Devil said to Him, "I will give You all this domain and its glory; for it has been handed over to me, and I give it to whomever I wish. Therefore if You worship before me, it shall all be Yours." Jesus answered him, "It is written, 'You shall worship the LORD your God and serve Him only.'" (Luke 4:5–8)

Perhaps Satan transported Jesus to the mountains of Moab where He could see the caravans moving along the great trade routes from all the nations of the known world. As Satan showed Jesus the kingdoms of the world and all their glory, he was offering the Son of Man a political messiahship. It's what the Jews were expecting. It's what they wanted. So Satan baited Him: "Go ahead, Jesus, give them what they want. Accommodate your message to the expectations of the people."

The irony of it all is that as God's Son, Jesus had a divine right to all the kingdoms of the world—and at the end of time, He will take His rightful place on the throne. Satan was simply suggesting that Jesus circumvent the Father's timetable.

So Satan appealed to the lust of the eyes. "Jesus, do You like what You see? Don't You wish You had control of all that? I can give it to You. You don't have to go to the cross. You don't have to suffer. Why wait for what You can have now? Why submit to being a servant when You can reign as King now? I am merely offering You a shortcut to what Your Father has already promised You."

Satan wasn't offering Jesus something he didn't have—this temptation was no bluff. The Devil is the god of this age and the head of this world's system. "We are of God," John reminds us, "and . . . the whole world lies in the power of the evil one" (1 John 5:19). This offer was consistent with Satan's methods of enticing Eve, David and others down through the centuries. The Enemy appealed to delights, desires and pleasures. "Take a look. What do You think? It's all Yours if You will worship me. You can cut a few corners to satisfy your desires. Just kiss the ring and bow at my feet."

The true nature of this temptation is found in the original language of Luke 4:5–6. The phrase "in a moment in time" is derived from the Greek word *stigma*, the same word used to describe the beatings Christ would receive. The phrase "for it has been handed over to me" is the same wording used when Jesus was "handed over" to be cru-

This offer was consistent with Satan's methods down through the centuries. The enemy appealed to delights, desires and pleasures.

cified (see Matt. 26:45). So here's the crux of the temptation: "Jesus, you can have the glory without the cross. No stigma, no betrayal, no being handed over. You can have all the gain with none of the pain."

But there was a price tag attached. The Devil was not inviting Jesus to abandon His mission altogether, but to fulfill it in another way. He tempted the Lord to compromise in order to accomplish the plan. The lust of the eyes is always looking for ways to fulfill life on our terms with as little discomfort and sacrifice as possible.

Have you ever been tempted to compromise? Think about something you've really wanted—a car, certain clothes, someone's house, a new job, another person. The Devil will tell you, "I can get that for you. I can arrange that. Just one thing—you'll have to hand over control of your life to me."

The Enemy won't ask you to abandon your faith, but he will compel you to compromise, cut corners and water down your faith. He will assure you of no pain and all gain, but his promises are empty. He can't give you anything that lasts. What if he offers you fame, for instance? Andy Warhol said we all get fifteen minutes of fame, but I think he was overestimating! Fame is fleeting. Can you remember who won the Super Bowl or the World Series last year? How about the winners of the Academy Awards five years ago? John's admonition rings true to this day: "The world is passing away, and also its lusts; but the one who does the will of God lives forever" (1 John 2:17).

We are all tempted to cut corners in our efforts to climb the ladder of success. We have all wanted to be the "the big man on campus" or the homecoming queen. Someone asked Chuck Colson why anyone would want to be president of the United States. Colson answered with one word: "POWER!"

The seed of Satan's rebellion was birthed in a desire to control. He wanted to run the show. Years ago I wrote down these points in my Bible that describe our adversary:

- His master passion is found in Isaiah 14:14—to be "like the Most High."
- His master perversion is found in Genesis 3:5—"you will be like God."
- His main desire is found in Luke 4:7—"worship before me."
- His main motive is found in 2 Thessalonians 2:4—"who opposes and exalts himself above every so-called god or object of worship, so that he takes his seat in the temple of God, displaying himself as being God."

Whatever you worship you will ultimately serve. Jesus declared to the Devil His intention to worship His heavenly Father and serve Him only. He refused to cut corners. He was here to change the eternal destiny of the human race for all time. The Father had a game plan, and Christ would one day rule over the kingdoms of the world, at the appointed time. Being eternal, Jesus wasn't in a hurry.

If you want to overcome the lust of the eyes, make some decisions right now. First, make a decision about sin (see Rom. 6:2). Next, make a decision about your goals in life (see Phil. 1:21). Finally, make a decision about your allegiance (see Rom. 6:11–14).

I heard a story of a man who wanted to sell his house. Another man wanted to buy it, but he couldn't afford the full price. After days of bargaining, the owner agreed to sell the house for half the original price with one small stipulation in the contract. The seller would retain ownership of one small nail protruding over the front door. After a few years the original owner decided he wanted to move back into his old house, but the new owner was unwilling to sell. So the original owner acted on the fine print in the contract. He found the carcass of a dead dog and hung it on the nail he still owned. The house became unlivable, and the family was forced to sell it to the owner of the nail. If you compromise with the Devil and leave him even one small opening in your life, he will make every effort to reclaim his property.

The Pride of Life

Finally, Satan appeals to our pride. When Satan comes at Jesus for the knockout punch, he doesn't hesitate.

And he led Him to Jerusalem and had Him stand on the pinnacle of the temple, and said to Him, "If You are the Son of God, throw Yourself down from here; for it is written, 'He will command His angels concerning You to guard You,' and 'On their hands they will bear You up, so that You will not strike Your foot against a stone.'" And Jesus answered and said to him, "It is said, 'You shall not put the LORD your God to the test.'" And when the Devil had finished every temptation, he departed from Him until an opportune time. (Luke 4:9–13)

Satan is relentless as he increases the pressure. Don't overlook where he took our Lord—to the heart of the nation, Jerusalem; to the heart of the city, the temple; to the highest point of the temple, the pinnacle. Jesus loved Jerusalem. He would minister in the streets, perform miracles and weep over its people. The temptation was simple: "Since it's only a matter of time before you start your miracle-working business, why not start now?"

The Devil pulled out Psalm 91, knowing the verses would resonate with Christ. "For He will command His angels concerning you, to guard you in all your ways. They will bear you up in their hands, that you do not strike your foot against a stone" (91:11–12). Here's the Devil's subtle twist: Since Jesus was going to live by the Word of God, He should be confronted by the Word of God. Satan put Jesus to a Bible test. "If You won't use Your miraculous powers to help Yourself, at least let Your Father show how much He loves You. Let Him reveal His power on Your behalf. Go ahead, Jesus, jump off the temple. Your Father won't let You fall."

The temptation was to do something dramatic and he-

roic. Even in the eyes of the most skeptical Jews, this would
have been proof that Jesus was the Messiah. So Satan prods
Him: "Aren't you willing to
take God at His word? Throw

To test God is to doubt Him.
To doubt God is to disbelieve
Him. And unbelief is sin.

yourself down. Prove to all Israel that you are the Promised
One. Prove that Your Father
can be trusted." Isn't it true
that we are in awe of the spectacular? We love big shows, big
events, big fireworks and big concerts. In fact, the bigger the
better. This is the boastful pride of life.

G. Campbell Morgan wrote, "It is when we doubt a person that we make experiments to discover how far they are
to be trusted." To test God is to doubt Him. To doubt God
is to disbelieve Him. And unbelief is sin.

Jesus refused to abuse His Father's power to attract a
crowd. In the wilderness, man is put to the test, not God.
Jesus refused to be a sanctified stuntman. He didn't come to
prove Himself by walking on hot coals, putting his head in
the lion's mouth or leaping tall buildings in a single bound.

In reality the appeal to our pride is a temptation to test
God. This is what the children of Israel did—they put God
to the test (see Deut. 6:16). They were blessed, protected
and fed, but they complained and bellyached about their
conditions.

We are guilty of presumption when we use the Bible as a
proof-text and make demands of God. God honors His
Word, but He does not honor misuse or abuse of it. Scripture is not a magic wand we wave on a whim. Satan quoted
some verses from Psalm 91, but he left out verse 14: "Because he has loved Me, therefore I will deliver him; I will set

him securely on high, because he has known My name." God will not bless us or deliver us because we spew out a few verses. God's power is for those who love Him, not those who manipulate Scripture to puff themselves up.

The Bible is full of admonitions about pride:

- The fear of the LORD is to hate evil; pride and arrogance and the evil way and the perverted mouth, I hate. (Prov. 8:13)

- Everyone who is proud in heart is an abomintion to the LORD; assuredly, he will not be unpunished. (Prov. 16:5)

- Pride goes before destruction, and a haughty spirit before stumbling. (Prov. 16:18)

- Therefore it says, "God is opposed to the proud, but gives grace to the humble." (James 4:6)

Pride is the opposite of humility. Jesus approached His wilderness temptations with two things: the Spirit of God and a mind filled with the Word of God. He never used His position as the Son of God to overcome Satan. He used the same provisions that are available to us: the Spirit and the Word. So how can you develop convictions that will withstand the fires of temptation?

Be on guard. Learn the schemes of the Devil. There are no new tricks in his bag, and he plays his trump card early. He is possessed by lust and pride, so keep your armor on.

Be prepared. Jesus knew the Word. He didn't have to run to church to get the preacher's advice. And He didn't just quote Scripture, He lived it. His reactions reflect more than passing a Scripture memory class. He was obviously immersed in the Word.

Be discerning. Don't be naive. Don't say, "I'll never do that. It will never happen to me." Remember, "Let him who thinks he stands take heed that he does not fall" (1 Cor. 10:12).

The story is told of a revolution in which the heir apparent to the throne was taken hostage by the mobs. They thought they could torture him and tempt him to renounce his kingship. They placed him with the foulest people in the country and tried to destroy his character. Yet with each temptation and each prodding to do evil, he would stomp his feet and shout, "No! No! No! I was born to be a king!"

You are a child of the King. Don't let the world, your flesh or the Devil tell you differently.

Over time, sequoias drop their lower branches through wind, fire, lightning or by choice, laying aside childish, youthful things unfit for a mature tree. Even the upper branches are thinned out until only the strongest remain, strategically placed to absorb the maximum amount of sun and rain. They know what is important for sustaining life and purpose.

*Trust in the LORD with all your heart
and do not lean on your own understanding. In all your ways acknowledge Him, and He will make your
paths straight.*
(Prov. 3:5–6)

6

Fireproof Your Decision-making

MY WIFE TERRI is a great teacher and very discerning. While recently teaching a group of pastors' wives,
she told them it concerns her when she hears a Christian say,
"Well, I have a peace about it," or, "It all worked out smoothly,
so it must have been God's will."

That, of course, is not necessarily the case. God's will
does not always take us down an easy road. We can't have
the peace of God if we aren't obedient to the will and Word
of God. Any peace we experience apart from obedience is a
false sense of security that comes from lying to ourselves.

During my senior year of college, I was trying to decide
where to attend seminary, and a friend suggested I visit Midwestern Seminary in Kansas City. One weekend Terri and I
and another couple drove through the night to Midwestern.
We enjoyed our time there and met some wonderful people.
We believed God was leading us to Midwestern.

Our decision made no sense, however, to a lot of people,
especially our families. Midwestern was over twenty hours

from home and family, and we only knew one couple there. We would have to pay for it ourselves without any outside financial assistance. People thought we were crazy, and we probably were. New Orleans Baptist Theological Seminary offered me a full scholarship, but I didn't believe that was God's plan for us. It would have been the easy path because everyone seemed to go to New Orleans Seminary when they left south Mississippi. I was certain, though, that it wasn't God's path for us.

When it came time to move, we had just $450 in our bank account. The day we were to leave, I had two cavities filled. That morning the car wouldn't start, and it died again while on the way home from the dentist. We had it towed, and it was hit by another car on the way to the shop. Finally, late that afternoon, we loaded up and headed out in our rental truck and dented car.

About two and a half hours out of town, the engine on the truck blew up. We had to transfer all our belongings, such as they were, to a new truck. We finally found a hotel and collapsed on the bed, exhausted. Terri looked at me and said, "Just say it again: You are SURE we are supposed to move to Kansas City?"

The transition was hard. We weren't prepared for a harsh Missouri winter in our light-weight clothing. Terri got a job downtown, but had to ride the bus to work, which cut into our already meager budget. Things were so tight financially that if some visiting friends hadn't brought the turkey, we would have eaten SPAM® for our first Thanksgiving at Midwestern.

But it wasn't all bad. I met many people in Kansas City who made a great impact on my life. I met Charlie Draper, who became my first pastor when I left seminary. Charlie taught me how to study the Word. I also met Ron Dunn and heard the great missionary, Bertha Smith, during those days. We were often hungry and cold, but we wouldn't trade our time there for anything.

Following the will of God doesn't make us exempt from trouble. The book of James tells us not to be surprised when we face trials because they are an inevitable part of life. If you are alive, you will face trials. The question comes in your response: Are you going to seek the will of God or try to convince God that your will and way are best?

By faith I can know that "all things . . . work together for good" (Rom. 8:28), even when I can't see how. I can trust God to show me His will. By faith and wisdom I see the heart and mind of God and trust in His purpose and plan for my life. Even when things go wrong, I can know that God has not abandoned His purpose. As Warren Wiersbe has often said, "We don't live by explanations, we live by promises."

Following the will of God doesn't make us exempt from trouble. If you are alive, you will face trials.

God's Guidance Is Sure

If you are seeking God's will, at some point someone is bound to tell you that you've made the wrong decision. There are people who second-guessed the prophets for speaking out so much. They questioned Jesus when He said it wasn't time to go to Jerusalem. Then they questioned Him when

He said it *was* time to go to Jerusalem. I'm sure someone told Martin Luther to keep his ninety-five theses to himself. They told William Carey not to go to the mission field. I imagine they told D.L. Moody that an uneducated man can't start a college. "They" are often wrong.

It would be out of character for God to leave us without directions. The One who sets the stars on their course, who made the universe, who put all things in order—would He then create man and leave us to guess about what He wants us to do?

In considering God's willingness to guide us, I believe there are several things we can know for sure: 1) God loves us unconditionally; we can trust a God like that. 2) God wants to speak to us and guide us through His Word. 3) God's Spirit will confirm the Word and guide us into all truth. 4) God has a purpose for our lives and doesn't want us to miss it.

If God cared enough to die for us, He cares enough to guide us. Think about it:

- God led Noah to build the ark.
- God led Abraham to leave his comfort zone and set out for a new land.
- God led Joseph even when it didn't seem like God was anywhere to be found. Joseph said to his brothers, "You meant it for evil, but God meant it for good."
- God led His people out of Egypt and into the Promised Land.
- God led Samuel to anoint a shepherd boy named David.
- God led Paul to carry the gospel to the Gentiles.

It's not that we don't want to know the will of God, but sometimes we are afraid of what God might want us to do. We may even think that God's will means doing something we dislike. Somehow we have bought the lie that following God might not work out for our good. Much of what Christians really believe about the will of God has no Biblical basis.

Another error we can make is believing that a bad decision in our past will keep us from finding God's will today. Jeremiah reminds us that when God finds a flawed and marred vessel, He doesn't throw it away; He remakes it. Never put a limit on what God can do if you'll get back in step with Him.

I've met people who assume that a closed door today is a closed door forever. But God's delay is not always His denial. It may be a matter of timing.

Yielding to the will of God is nothing less than giving God rule of your life. It's not about being willing to do a particular thing; it's being willing to do anything God asks of you.

Obedience to the revealed will of God is not optional. Don't waste your time trying to negotiate or bargain with God. If you take that path, you are going to be hurt. John Calvin said, "God cannot approve of anything that is not supported by His Word."

God's Word Is Our Compass

In 2008, Sir Edmund Hillary died at age 88. Hillary was the first to scale the 29,035-foot summit of Mount Everest, the world's tallest peak. In the annals of exploits and exploration, it is one of the great events of history. His climb ranks with the first trek to the South Pole by Roald Amundsen in 1911 and the first solo nonstop trans-Atlantic flight by Charles Lindbergh in 1927.

All three men had something in common: They used a compass to direct their course. Boy Scouts and famous explorers alike use this simple tool to keep their bearings. The compass for fireproofing our decisions is the Word of God. It is the basis for guidance and direction.

God's will revealed in God's Word is His best for us. Satan wants to deceive us into thinking it's not. The Enemy and our flesh will want us to rely on feelings. God never does His deep work in the shallowest part of our being. Feelings can deceive us. We may think we know what is best, but often we are wrong.

God's will revealed in God's Word is His best for us. Satan wants to deceive us into thinking it's not.

The best way to fireproof your life is to bathe your decision-making in the Word of God. He never guides you to make a decision inconsistent with His Word.

As we seek God's will in our decisions, the Lord makes many areas of His purpose clear. It is a mistake to think God hides His will from us and that somehow we are left to figure it out on our own. In many cases fireproof decision-making is as simple as obeying the clear instructions of Scripture. The Bible tells us that it is God's will for us to be saved, Spirit-filled, sanctified, submissive to authority and sexually pure, among other things.

Let's be honest, the parts of the Bible we have the most trouble with are not the parts we don't understand, but the parts we do understand. These are non-negotiable no-brainers:

- Obey your parents. (Eph. 6:1)
- Don't marry an unbeliever. (2 Cor. 6:14)
- Give of your resources. (2 Cor. 8–9)
- Live a life of praise. (1 Thess. 5:16)
- Pray. (1 Thess. 5:17)
- Support your family. (1 Tim. 5:8)
- Gather with other believers in a local church. (Heb. 10:25)

You don't have to pray to know what God wants in these areas. They are clearly stated as the desire of God in Scripture.

A Compass for Personal Direction

There are personal issues in our lives which the Bible does not address. There is nothing specific in God's Word about owning a television, listening to the radio, what kind of house you should live in or what career path you should choose. How do we make decisions that glorify God in these areas? Here are some basic questions to ask yourself to make sure your life aligns with Scripture:

- Will it lead to a deeper love for Christ and greater maturity?
- Does it have the power to control me?
- What are my motives?
- Will it violate the Lordship of Christ in my life?
- Will it be a positive witness to the lost or other believers?

Though God's Word does not give us specifics about many of our day-to-day choices and decisions, it assures us that the Lord will lead us in our personal lives:

- I will instruct you and teach you in the way which you should go; I will counsel you with My eye upon you. (Ps. 32:8)
- Trust in the LORD with all your heart and do not lean on your own understanding. In all your ways acknowledge Him, and He will make your paths straight. (Prov. 3:5–6)
- Your ears will hear a word behind you, "This is the way, walk in it," whenever you turn to the right or to the left. (Isa. 30:21)
- Thus says the LORD, your Redeemer, the Holy One of Israel, "I am the LORD your God, who teaches you to profit, who leads you in the way you should go." (Isa. 48:17)

George Müller wrote,

I never remember in all my Christian life that I ever sincerely and patiently sought to know the will of God by the teaching of the Spirit, through the Word, without being directed clearly and rightly. But if honesty of heart and uprightness before God were lacking, or if I did not patiently wait upon God for instruction, or if I preferred the counsel of my fellow men to the declaration of the Word of the living God, I made great mistakes.

Müller had a simple method for determining how to make right decisions:

I seek at the beginning to get my heart into such a state that it has no will of its own in regard to a given matter. Nine-tenths of the trouble with people generally is just here.

Nine-tenths of the difficulties are overcome when our hearts are ready to do the LORD's will, whatever it may be. When one is truly in this state, it is usually but a little way to the knowledge of what His will is.

Having done this, I do not leave the result to feeling or simple impression. If so, I make myself liable to great delusions.

I seek the Will of the Spirit of God through, or in connection with, the Word of God. The Spirit and the Word must be combined. If I look to the Spirit alone without the Word, I lay myself open to great delusions also. If the Holy Ghost guides us at all, He will do it according to the Scriptures and never contrary to them.

Next I take into account providential circumstances. These often plainly indicate God's Will in connection with His Word and Spirit.

I ask God in prayer to reveal His Will to me aright.

Thus, through prayer to God, the study of the Word, and reflection, I come to a deliberate judgment according to the best of my ability and knowledge, and if my mind is thus at peace, and continues so after two or three more petitions, I proceed accordingly. In trivial matters, and in transactions involving most important issues, I have found this method always effective.[1]

Making fireproof decisions begins and ends with a desire to do the will of God. Safe decision-making will never happen if we try to convince the Father to see things our way.

Ron Dunn preached the best message on finding God's will I've ever heard. It was based on Romans 12:1–2. He ended

> *Making fireproof decisions begins and ends with a desire to do the will of God.*

that message with three guidelines.

The first is desire. "Delight yourself in the LORD; and He will give you the desires of your heart" (Ps. 37:4). If we are committed to delighting ourselves in the Lord, we can assume that our delight, His desires and our desires will line up.

The second guideline is opportunity. Desire alone is not enough. Some of our own desires can be selfish, but desires that come from God are always accompanied by an open door. Where He guides, He provides. God's leading begins with desire and is confirmed by opportunity.

The final guideline is learned from Balaam's donkey: We must go forward with humility, leaning on God for continued clarity. Balaam tried to justify his actions. He talked himself into believing something was right that wasn't. Ron said, "I feel right. I have a peace. But if I've misread my own heart, if it's not Your will, I don't want it. I'm watching for barriers and obstacles." When in doubt, don't.

There are no distinctions between big and little issues in the will of God. From our perspective we might think a certain decision is no big deal, but the magnitude of that decision may affect us years down the road.

All of us have made decisions we regret. Maybe you've made a poor choice in your life and still bear the scars today. The choices you make now affect you for the rest of your life. Even the most godly people make wrong choices. But some people think the will of God is like Humpty Dumpty— a wrong choice in one area means they are forever broken and can never put their lives back together again. Nothing could be further from the truth!

Maybe you've blown it in your career choice, in a relationship or a financial decision. Maybe you've been burned. You can't change the past, but you can do something to safe-guard yourself in the days ahead.

John Wesley, revivalist and founder of Methodism, is an example of a man who struggled to know the will of God for his personal life, yet who was greatly used to bring many to Christ.

Fearing marriage would distract him from ministry, he still found himself drawn, at the age of thirty-two, to a young lady he met while serving in Georgia. After drawing an "answer" from a hat, he concluded he was to "think of it no more." Later in life he fell in love with another woman, but was influenced to avoid matrimony in this case, as well.

Finally, in his late forties, Wesley married a wealthy widow named Mary Vazeille. It was a very unhappy marriage and she eventually left him. Wesley wrote in his journal, "I have not left her; I would not send her away; I will not recall her."[2]

Obviously, God used Wesley even though he had a terrible and tragic marriage. Finding the will of God is not about waving a magic wand or seeing what the majority of your friends think. How do you know the will of God? How can you fireproof the decisions of your life? We won't always make perfect decisions, but we can have a biblical approach to decision-making.

If we get right down to it and can't discern what the good, acceptable and perfect will of God is for our lives, the following questions will likely pinpoint the trouble:

Do you believe that God's will can be known definitely and accurately? (Ps. 32:8, Isa. 30:21)

Are you willing to seek God's will and do it, or would you just like to know it as an option? (John 7:17)

Have you made a permanent decision of commitment to be yielded to God for the rest of your life? (Rom. 12:1–2)

Is there any known unconfessed sin in your life? If so, stop here and confess it and forsake it. (Ps. 66:18, Prov. 28:13, 1 John 1:9)

Are you obeying the known will of God for your life on a daily basis? If not, start today and demonstrate your obedience before going on. (Ps. 119:59–60)

Are you in neutral? Are you willing to go either way on this issue? Ask God that His desires will be your desires. (Phil. 2:13)

Are you praying specifically and definitely about it in faith? Make a list of your specific thoughts and pray about them by faith. (Mark 10:51, James 1:5–7)

Are you spending time with God daily in prayer and Bible study? If not, begin today. (Ps. 5:3)

Have you asked the counsel of three spiritually mature people? (Prov. 11:14, 12:15, 15:22, 19:20, 20:18, 24:6)

Are you willing to wait in faith for God to line up His Word, your peace and the circumstances? (Heb. 10:36)

Do you have an inner conviction or peace about your course of action? (Rom. 14:23)

Will it bring glory to God? (1 Cor. 10:31, Col. 3:17)

The Test of Our Decisions

In life we have tests, fire drills if you will, that give us an opportunity to make a God-honoring decision. When we study the life of Abraham, we realize God used every test to grow Abraham in his faith.

In Genesis 22:1–10 God put Abraham to the ultimate test. The command of God to offer up Isaac was as real as it gets. It's easy to say we want to honor God in our decision-making, but the reality of our words is revealed when the test hits close to home.

Whereas Satan tempts us in order to lead us to do evil, God tests us to bring out the best in us. Abraham's test involved the heir to the promise, the joy of his life. Here we see a man who teaches that we can love God and make right decisions even when His leading appears to be illogical or costly. I heard Vance Havner say, "When we go through God's testing properly, all we lose are the shackles that tied us up earlier."

Have you considered that God's tests are evidence that He trusts us—or more accurately, He trusts Himself to keep us? His intention is not that our faith will fail, but develop. We should remember that God always prepares us for the test. Genesis 22:1 says, "Now it came about after these things . . ." What things? All the other tests. God didn't want Isaac's life; He wanted Abraham's heart.

It's easy to say we want to honor God in our decision-making, but the reality of our words is revealed when the test hits close to home.

Look at Abraham's decision-making process. When God told him to sacrifice his son, he responded immediately. He didn't wait, argue or negotiate. Abraham obeyed. Someone has said, "True spirituality is often measured by the length of response time to God's commands." This is where many believers get hung up and ultimately get derailed. But Abraham obeyed because he believed God. "We will worship and we will come back . . . God will provide."

Typically we go through tests in the area of our possessions (how we use them), our plans (how we yield them)
and people (how we treat them). It is doubtful that God can
use us in a significant way until we have passed these tests.
It's meaningless to pray, "God, use me," if we aren't willing
for God to make us usable.

When we think about Abraham, we can observe a powerful truth: Whatever we cling to is usually what God asks
for.

Ron Dunn preached a classic message on this passage in
which he said, "Isaac was God's idea, now He's going to take
him away. In verse two, God is twisting the knife. 'Thy son,
thy only son, Isaac, whom you love . . .' Isaac was the culmi-
nation of God's work and plan. Isaac was spared. God never
intended for Isaac to die. Somebody died on that mountain;
it was Abraham. He had to die to Isaac. God knew until He
had Isaac, He didn't have all of Abraham. Until Isaac was on
the altar, God was not on the throne."

We say we want to make godly decisions, but all too
often, in reality we don't want to give up the thing that is
our pride and joy. We must become like Abraham, voluntar-
ily and deliberately choosing the will of God.

A sixteenth-century believer wrote,

> After having given myself wholly to God . . . I renounced,
> for the love of Him, everything that was not He; and I be-
> gan to live as if there were none but He and I in the world
> . . . I made this my business . . . I drove away from my mind
> everything that was capable of interrupting my thought of
> God . . . When we are faithful to keep ourselves in His holy
> presence, and set Him always before us, this not only hin-
> ders our offending Him, and doing anything that may dis-

please Him . . . but it also begets in us a holy freedom . . . a familiarity with God, wherewith we ask, and that successfully, the graces we stand in need of . . . These acts . . . become habitual, and the presence of God is rendered as it were natural to us.[3]

The longevity of this remarkable tree is more impressive than its size. The giant sequoia keeps its youth far longer than any of its neighbors. The silver firs are old in their second or third century, pines in their fourth or fifth, but the big tree growing beside them is still in the bloom of its youth, growing in every feature when the pines have gotten old.

Catch the foxes for us, the little foxes
that are ruining the vineyards.
(Song of Sol. 2:15)

7

Fireproof Your Marriage

MARRIAGE IS hard work, but people don't always work hard at it. Many of those who "tie the knot" get "untied" within the first few years. Celebrating a fiftieth, or even a twenty-fifth, wedding anniversary is rare these days, and divorce rates are as high among Christians as non-believers. John Leo writes,

> One of the problems in trying to shore up the institution of marriage is that so many of the professionals who teach and write about it—counselors, therapists, academics, and popular authors—really don't support marriage at all. Some depict it as archaic and inherently oppressive. Others give it tepid support as just one of many acceptable adult arrangements.[1]

We have allowed the postmodern mindset to convince our churches and our couples that divorce is now the norm rather than an exception. Divorce is not God's solution. God allows divorce under specific and limited terms and only because of the sinfulness and hardness of man's heart. When marriage is no longer compatible with the culture, the culture needs to change, not the institution of marriage.

In the movie *Fireproof,* Caleb and Catherine Holt have been married for seven years. Although once in love, they have grown apart and find themselves headed for divorce. Tension fills the air in every conversation. Their self-centeredness leads to countless arguments in which they indulge in finger-pointing and exaggerating one another's shortcomings. In reality they lack something or someone to hold them together and to restore their lost love—that someone is Jesus Christ. Only when Caleb finds Christ and begins to love his wife the way Christ loves the church do the tables begin to turn.

> *When marriage is no longer compatible with the culture, the culture needs to change, not the institution of marriage.*

At one point in the movie Caleb has come to Christ, but Catherine is still skeptical. She has seen a change, but she's not sure why and even doubts his motives. One day while Catherine is sick in bed, Caleb brings her medicine and begins to open his heart to her.

Caleb: Can you take this medicine and eat something?

Catherine: Why are you doing this?

Caleb: Because I've learned that you don't leave your partner, especially in a fire.

Catherine: What's happened to you?

Caleb: Dad asked me if there was anything in me that wanted to save our marriage, and he gave me this notebook. He said it saved their marriage.

Catherine: So what day are you on [in the notebook]?

Caleb: 43.

Catherine: But there's only 40 days in the book.

Caleb: Who says I have to stop?

Catherine: Caleb, I don't know how to process this. This is not normal for you.

Caleb: Welcome to the new normal.

Catherine: You didn't want to do this at first, did you?

Caleb: No, but halfway through I realized that I never really understood what love was. Once I figured that out, I wanted to do it.

Catherine: Caleb, I want to believe this is real, but I'm not ready to say I trust you again.

Caleb: I understand. But whether you get to that point or not, I need you to know something. Catherine, I'm sorry . . . I have been so selfish. For the last seven years I've trampled on you with my words and my actions. I've loved other things when I should have loved you. In the last few weeks God has given me a love for you that I've never had before. I've asked Him to forgive me and have been hoping . . . praying that you would somehow be able to forgive me too. I don't want

Caleb introduces Catherine to the "new normal" and seeks her forgiveness for his past mistakes.

to live the rest of my life without you.

Catherine: Caleb, I'm supposed to give the divorce papers back to my lawyer next week. I need some time to think.

Caleb: You can have all the time you need.

A Distorted View

Maybe you are at the point of giving up on your marriage. You may be living under the same roof with your spouse, in a house that's not a home. How do you survive? How do you restore the love you once had? How do you make the choice to never leave your partner behind, especially in a fire?

If you have ever suffered a divorce, you know from experience that there's no such thing as a divorce without scars. I have friends and family members who still carry the scars of divorce and its lingering consequences. As a youth minister I saw the effect that broken homes have on kids, and as a pastor I know the agony of watching a couple separate.[2]

When a couple lets conflict get out of control, emotional tension builds. Anger and frustration replace affection, and a root of bitterness begins to grow. Concerns become complaints, complaints become threats, and threats lead to disaster. Suddenly there's nothing in the home but name calling, put-downs and cutting remarks.

Once a couple starts down this path, they begin to withdraw and shut down emotionally. They may even begin to sleep in separate rooms. Intervention may be needed to change their direction. But once the couple starts thinking of or threatening divorce, problems escalate to a whole new level.

Contemporary culture only contributes to the problem because society's view of marriage is about as far as you can get from a life-long commitment based on a covenant with God. One Hollywood couple's marriage lasted fifteen days. A couple married more than ten years in Hollywood is a rarity. Now the church is following that lead. At a lot of wedding ceremonies, couples say "as long as our love shall last" in place of "till death do us part."

A Solemn Vow

When a man and a woman face one other and repeat their vows during a wedding ceremony, it is not just meaningless ritual. They are making a promise before God and those gathered, and it should be taken seriously. Solomon wrote, "When you make a vow to God, do not be late in paying it; for He takes no delight in fools. Pay what you vow! It is better that you should not vow than that you should vow and not pay" (Eccl. 5:4–5).

Yet many couples come to the altar completely unaware that they are making a solemn oath, and with no expectation that the marriage will last. Solomon's strong warning reminds us that a vow is intended to be permanent. Chuck Swindoll writes, "No amount of psychological therapy, positive thinking (often dubbed 'grace'), semantic footwork with a biblical text, alternative concepts or mutual support from family and friends can remove your responsibility to keep your vow."[3] The story has often been told that Ruth

> *Marriage is a covenant before God—an agreement that is not based on the faithfulness of the people involved, but on God's faithfulness.*

Graham was asked if she had ever considered divorcing Billy. She responded, "Murder, yes; divorce, no."

False Information

One reason society takes divorce lightly is because we've bought the Devil's lie that marriage is merely a human contract. In reality, marriage is a covenant before God—an agreement that is not based on the faithfulness of the people involved, but on God's faithfulness to fulfill His covenant obligations. Marriage is a unique relationship between three people: God, the man and the woman. When a Christian couple lives as God designed, they are a powerful witness for the gospel.

Tertullian, the second-century martyr, said,

> How beautiful is the marriage of two Christians, two who are one in hope, desire, one in the way of life they follow, one in the religion they practice . . . nothing divides them, either in flesh or spirit. They pray together, worship together, fast together, instructing one another. Side by side they visit God's church and partake of God's banquet; side by side they face difficulties and persecution and share their consolations. They have no secrets from one another; they never shun each other's company, they never bring sorrow to each other's hearts. They visit the sick and assist the needy. Psalms and hymns they sing to one another. Hearing and seeing this, Christ rejoices. To such as these He gives peace.[4]

There is nothing more powerful today than a Christian home built on Christian values and a Biblical worldview.

Another great lie of Satan about marriage, perpetrated

largely through the media, is that intimacy is limited to a sexual relationship. True intimacy, however, is a sharing of heart and mind between a couple.

When I was serving a church in Oklahoma, there was a couple in our congregation (now both gone to be with the Lord) that epitomized the love of a covenant marriage. The husband was blind and his wife was in terrible health, but the joy they shared was something to behold.

In fact, although he was blind, he would drive and she would be his eyes. She would tell him how fast he was going, where to turn and when to change lanes. While I would never condone such a dangerous practice, I have to admit it was a partnership like I've never seen.

Staying in Touch

Communication is a major key to marital intimacy. If you want your marriage to burn up quickly, just neglect communicating with one another. According to *New Man Magazine*, the typical U.S. married couple only spends four minutes a day in "meaningful conversation" with each other.[5] That's less than one percent of their waking hours!

The only way your spouse can know your thoughts and feelings is by communication. Years ago I heard the following statistic: Of the Christian couples that spend time together spiritually, only one in 400 will ever divorce. You can choose to invest in your marriage spiritually.

Every living thing—plants, animals, people, churches, marriages—needs nourishment to survive. When a couple communicates they are nourishing their marriage. If the husband loves his wife the way he loves himself, he will feed his marriage emotionally, physically, verbally and spiritually. Communication has nothing to do with being extroverted; it has to do with being the person God has called you to be.

Many of today's marriages lack intimacy. We need to seek the Lord as individuals and as couples. If marriage is a "holy estate," as the traditional wedding ceremony says, then God belongs front and center in our marriages. We need to talk about spiritual things and spend time together in prayer.

Little Foxes

In the Song of Solomon we read, "Catch the foxes for us, the little foxes that are ruining the vineyards" (2:15). Foxes get into vineyards to feed on the grapes, and the keepers must prop up the branches so the foxes can't reach them. Warren Wiersbe says that the "little foxes" represent those things that quietly destroy relationships.

> *Being inconsiderate leads to being ungrateful, and ingratitude will result in a preoccupation with lesser things.*

It only takes little things to come in and destroy something great. Most marriages fall apart because little things become big things. What seems unimportant now can become unmanageable down the road. Marital conflict over trivial issues has been the source of many jokes for comedians, but those whose marriages have been destroyed by fighting are not laughing.

One example of the "little foxes" of marriage is disrespect—it can turn a marriage made in heaven into a private little hell. If most of us were as disrespectful to our friends and co-workers as we are to our spouse, we would be lonely and out of a job.

Another "little fox" is inconsideration. We don't call during the day to see how our spouse is doing. We forget anniversaries, birthdays or other special moments. We are too busy to leave a note saying we love them or are praying for them. Being inconsiderate leads to being ungrateful, and ingratitude will result in a preoccupation with lesser things. We need to constantly direct our minds to things that are true, honorable, right, pure, lovely, of good report, excellent and full of praise (Phil. 4:8).

Criticism and complaining are more "little foxes" that undermine relationships. God clearly communicated His thoughts on murmuring in Exodus 16. Nothing eats away at a marriage like bad words and attitudes. When the home becomes a constant environment of pointing out flaws, there are destructive foxes eating away at the branches.

Another "little fox" that destroys more families than we can number is finances. Financial problems are a leading cause of divorce in our society. It's a short distance from "making money to live" to "living to make money."

One source of conflict between Caleb and Catherine in the movie *Fireproof* is the way they handle their money. He selfishly saves for a boat and is unwilling to part with his dream, even when they need money to help her ailing parents.

A "little fox" that has been attacking marriages in more recent years is mobility. Couples are moving every few years in order to meet job demands and keep up with society's expectations. The more we move the less connected we feel with each other. The mindset "we'll only be here a few years, then we'll move on" works against fostering meaningful friendships and getting involved in a church. All this leads to superficial living.

A few years ago, one of our deacons and his wife faced the mobility challenge. Chad and Suzanna had struggled with his desire for career advancement and their desire as a family for a stable home. As Chad strove for promotions, his company pushed him to pick up his young family and move. Chad and Suzanna didn't want to, but it seemed they had no choice if Chad were to achieve his career goals.

While delayed in the St. Louis airport during a business trip, Chad picked up a copy of the *New York Times*. The front-page article was entitled, "The Five-Bedroom, Six-Figure Rootless Life." Chad was gripped by the following:

> They have traded a home in one place for a job that could be anyplace. Relocated children do not know a hometown; their parents do not know where their funerals will be. There is little in the way of small-town ties or big-city amenities— grandparents and cousins, longtime neighbors, vibrant boulevards, homegrown shops—that let roots sink in deep.[6]

During this time, a local business came up for sale. As Chad and Suzanna talked, prayed and sought godly counsel, doors began to open. In addition, pressures began to escalate with Chad's company and a timeline was created for his career move. In the end, Chad walked away from his job at a major industry to purchase the business. God blessed this transition, faithfully providing everything they needed for success in this new endeavor.

Chad is now home most nights for dinner. Suzanna and the children are very involved in his business, often traveling with him on out-of-town trips. He has the freedom to attend school events like field day and music presentations and rarely misses his kids' activities. "We have an overwhelming peace just knowing where our kids will go to school, where we will go to church and that we are close to family," says Chad. As a pastor, I'm grateful for couples like Chad and Suzanna who are modeling Biblical priorities.

God's Order

One important way to fireproof your marriage, though often scorned today, is to maintain Biblical order. A significant danger in marriages is the reversal or confusion in the roles of the husband and wife. These familiar words of Scripture often go unheeded or misinterpreted:

> *The man is to be a reflection of how Christ loves His church . . . a picture of Christ in the home.*

Wives, be subject to your own husbands, as to the Lord. For the husband is the head of the wife, as Christ also is the head of the church, He Himself being the Savior of the body. But as the church is subject to Christ, so also the wives ought to be to their husbands in everything. Husbands, love your wives, just as Christ also loved the church and gave Himself up for her. (Eph. 5:22–25)

While the Bible teaches equality between men and women regarding value, it also teaches a divine order of authority for the family. This order places the man as primarily responsible to God for the family. The man is to be a reflection of how Christ loves His church. In other words, the husband should be a picture of Christ in the home.

One reason roles get reversed is that some men shirk their responsibility. They fail to lead in word or deed; they relinquish the spiritual leadership of their homes. These men then fail to be role models for their children. They can teach their kids to play, but can't teach them to pray.

A husband can neglect his responsibilities by spending his spare time hunting, fishing, playing ball or lying in front of the TV. Many feel they are too tired to help after a long day at work, but they fail to see that their wives have been working all day as well.

Headship is not a title, it's a responsibility—one that some men would rather not carry. Dr. Charles Sell writes, "Our homes need leadership. A power vacuum, not a power struggle, exists in most of them. The modern husband may be more apt to abdicate than abuse his position. Women are forced into taking responsibility they often don't want."[7]

In counseling couples, I've also seen some husbands who consider their wives nothing more than cooks and maids. They misuse their authority by bossing their wives around and acting like "submit" is the only word in the Bible. This can easily degenerate into an abusive situation in which the man acts like a dictator.

"Wives, submit" does not mean "husbands, dominate." God did not create Eve from Adam's feet to be trampled upon, nor from his head to rule over him. He made her from Adam's side, the nearest place to his heart, to be his helpmate and companion.

Healthy marriages model a right understanding of submission. A husband is to nourish and strengthen his wife as a leader among equals, and both are to submit to the Lord. As Christ leads and loves the church, so the husband is to lead and love his wife. I've never met a woman whose husband loved her as Christ loves the church who opposed the idea of loving submission.

In his commentary on Ephesians, Warren Wiersbe writes,

> The trouble is that many homes are not governed by God's Word—even homes where the members are professing Christians—and the consequences are tragic. . . . Too many marriages end in the divorce court, and nobody knows how many husbands and wives are emotionally divorced even though they share the same address. The poet William Cowper called the home "the only bliss of Paradise that hast survived the Fall," but too many homes are an outpost of hell instead of a parcel of paradise.[8]

Peter, writing to the first-century church, dealt with the issue of husbands and wives. In First Peter 3 the great apostle is not saying wives are slaves. Rather, he wanted the behavior of wives with unbelieving husbands to bring harmony to the home and be a witness to their unbelieving husbands. Although submission is taught in at least four books in the New Testament, it is a misunderstood subject that the world likes to nail us on. But most marital conflict results from failing to live by Biblical principles, and attacking, ignoring, misrepresenting or misinterpreting submission is not the solution to the problem.

For a marriage to be God's best, there has to be one leader. God's call for the wife to submit does not mean blind obedience or inferiority. For Christians, submission must be mutual. Paul wrote, "Submit to one another out of reverence for Christ" (Eph. 5:21, NIV).

The husband's role to love his wife as Christ loves the church is also widely ignored or misunderstood. James Dobson writes,

A man said, "I don't understand my wife. She has everything she could want—a dishwasher, a new dryer, a nice house. I've been faithful and I don't drink. But she's miserable. I can't figure out why." His love-starved wife would have traded everything for a single expression of genuine tenderness from her unromantic husband. Appliances do not build self-esteem; being somebody's sweetheart most certainly does.[9]

How about it, husbands? Are you considerate of your wife? Do you love her as Christ loves the church? As husbands we're commanded to live with our wives in an understanding way (1 Pet. 3:7). That means I'm to know my wife intimately—her temperament, her likes and dislikes, her personality, her gifts and talents. If I am going to fireproof my home, I need to know my wife better than I know myself. I must understand that she may be weaker physically, but she's still my life partner. I'm called by God to protect, honor and help her any way I can.

Terri and I have been married over thirty years and, like all couples, we've had difficult seasons. Most of them were my fault—I was insensitive, non-communicative or self-absorbed. But through thick and thin, she's been my best friend. I'd rather be with her than anyone else on the planet. I respect her opinions and I seek her advice. I don't always like what she tells me because she's honest, but she's honest because she loves me.

One more thought. Peter talks about being the right kind of husband so that our prayers aren't hindered (1 Pet. 3:7). This verse is incredibly clear on how we treat our wives. The

A right relationship with God depends on being right with others.

text reveals that Peter is talking specifically to men. A right relationship with God depends on being right with others. I can't expect God to bless me, use me or answer my prayers if I'm not treating my wife as He instructs me to.

A Fireproof Marriage

In closing, here are a few suggestions for keeping your relationship healthy:

- Husbands, take your wife out on a date regularly. Plan it, prepare for it and court her the way you did when you were dating. Wives, plan a surprise for him, such as preparing his favorite dinner.

- Watch your personal attractiveness. Once you are married, it doesn't mean you can let yourself go. Take care of yourself. Anything that was important while you were dating should still be important.

- Continue to be courteous. Husbands, open the door for your wife. Wives, say thanks when he does something for you. Write unexpected notes. Give each other gifts for no specific reason other than "just because."

- Be understanding of personal interests. Let him play golf. Let her go shopping.

- Never criticize your spouse in public.

- Don't go to sleep angry. Remember, nobody wins an argument—it's not a competition.

- Start a family campaign of thoughtfulness and kindness. Pray every day that you will model the fruit of the Spirit in your home.

- Turn off the TV. Guys, turn off the sports channel and have a conversation. Ladies, turn off the soap operas and don't expect your husband to be the hunk of the year. Television plants unrealistic expectations in our minds, steals time we could be spending with one another and clutters our minds with an unbiblical view of life, love and marriage.

- Turn control of your finances over to the Lord.

- Pray together that you can put down roots and have stability in your home.

Let's change the culture! Let's love one another the way Christ loved us. Let's make a commitment to build godly homes. Let's model a Christian marriage in front of our lost friends and family.

The sequoia does not attain prime size and beauty before 1,500 years or become old before 3,000 years. Millennium after millennium, whatever the forces may deliver, sequoias triumph over tempest and fire and time, fruitful and beautiful, giving food and shelter to multitudes of small creatures dependent on their bounty.

For where your treasure is, there your heart will be also.
(Matt. 6:21)

8

Fireproof Your Finances

A CRITICAL AREA in which Satan constantly seeks a foothold in our lives is finances. A Christian who will not obey God in the area of money finds it harder to resist sin in other areas of life and is a poor witness for Christ. The writer of Proverbs said, "Honor the LORD from your wealth and from the first of all your produce; so your barns will be filled with plenty and your vats will overflow with new wine" (3:9–10). Giving back to God is the first principle of godly financial planning.

Several years ago I preached a series of messages called "Putting Your Financial House in Order." During that series, I shared a story I heard from John Maxwell. A father took his young son to a fast food restaurant for lunch. When asked what he wanted to eat, the little boy said, "I want French fries." The father placed the order and even super-sized the meal. They found a table, said the blessing and started eating. The dad finished his meal first, then reached for one of his son's fries. The boy put his arms over the fries and said defiantly, "These are MY fries!"

Such a selfish attitude shows that the little boy forgot a few things. First of all, he forgot that his father was the source of the fries: His dad took him to the restaurant, paid for the food and even carried the tray. He also forgot that his father didn't need his son's French fries; he could have bought his own. Finally, the son forgot that his dad had generously chosen to super-size the order. He did it because he loved his son.

> *Our God is a giving God. His greatest expression of giving is not found in possessions but in the person of Jesus Christ.*

The lesson is obvious. The dad didn't really want or need the fries, but he wanted his son to be grateful enough to share them willingly.

God Is a Giver

Since the dawning of creation, God has modeled giving for us:

- He gave Adam and Eve a beautiful garden to live in.
- He gave Israel a pillar of cloud for protection, a pillar of fire for guidance and manna from heaven for provision.
- He gave Israel the Promised Land.
- He gave a kingship to David, a lowly shepherd boy.
- He gave us His Son to die in our place.
- He gave us the indwelling Holy Spirit.

Our God is a giving God. His greatest expression of giving is not found in possessions but in the person of Jesus Christ. Christ continues to give to us through His love, mercy, forgiveness, grace, peace and power. We are debtors to God, and we owe Him everything.

If we want to follow the example of our heavenly Father, giving is not an option. Yet one area where believers kick and scream the most is stewardship. If we don't get that right, we'll never live abundant lives.

My parents were not rich people. My dad was a pharmacist. He owned his own store for a number of years until he had to close the doors. It so happened that the year he did, I was headed to a private college to begin studying for the ministry. I learned something about the faithfulness of God from my dad during that time.

My dad had taught me never to go into debt. He also taught me to tithe. He gave 25–30% of his income to the church. He didn't always agree with the preacher, but he knew he was giving his gift to the Lord. Another principle my dad taught me was sacrifice. He knew God had called me into the ministry, and he sacrificed greatly so I could go to college. I am indebted to my dad for teaching me these truths early in life.

Today, Terri and I give more than a tithe. We not only tithe to our church, but we also give sacrificially to our building program and other ministries. We give "over and above" for the joy of giving. Every Sunday, even after paying our tithes and offerings, we put something more in the plate in both services. We just don't want to come to church empty-handed. I'm learning the lesson that all I have is a sacred trust. None of it is mine; it all belongs to Him.

Giving Ourselves

Now, before you skip over this chapter, let me plead with you to take these truths to heart. This issue is crucial to the Christian life. Stewardship is lordship. This principle is captured in the story of a little boy who saw the offering plate going by. He didn't have any money, so he tore off a part of the bulletin and scribbled on it, "I give myself."

This is exactly what the Macedonian believers did. Paul wrote to the Corinthians and told them about the Macedonian church:

> Now, brethren, we wish to make known to you the grace of God which has been given in the churches of Macedonia, that in a great ordeal of affliction their abundance of joy and their deep poverty overflowed in the wealth of their liberality. For I testify that according to their ability, and beyond their ability, they gave of their own accord, begging us with much urging for the favor of participation in the support of the saints, and this, not as we had expected, but *they first gave themselves* to the Lord and to us by the will of God. (2 Cor. 8:1–5)

It's a blessing to see a people so committed to the work of God.

An angel in Milton's classic, *Paradise Lost*, could, by the touch of a certain spear, reveal the true character of a person. Similarly, the way we think about and use money gives good insight into who we really are. We may not give money away, but money will give us away.

If we don't learn to have God's perspective on our finances, we will make mammon our god, and all that we earn or own will one day be burned up. We must learn to lay up treasure in heaven where the fluctuating stock market, oil prices, thieves and scam artists can't get to it, or all we'll do is prepare for a big bonfire or yard sale one day.

I did a funeral years ago for a man whose family spent lavishly for his funeral. They bought the most expensive mahogany casket and copper vault—investing tens of thousands of dollars to be covered with dirt. As far as I could tell, the man had never invested in eternal things.

I've watched others, even people in the church, buy houses and lands while never laying up treasures in heaven. It is possible to come to church and sing songs about God, but refuse Him entry into our wallets.

You Can't Outgive God

What we do with our money represents who we are—our time, toil and talent. Someone once said, "Money is concentrated personality, or personality in coin. Our picture may not be on any bill, but our person is certainly in it." If our attitude and actions do not follow the example of the Macedonians, we'll have nothing to show for our lives when we get to heaven.

In his book, *As You Sow*, Bill Bright wrote the following:

> Many years ago, Dr. Oswald Smith, the famous Canadian evangelist and missionary statesman, spoke on stewardship to his congregation. "You can't beat God at giving," he said. "If you will deal honorably with God in money matters, obeying the command to bring all the tithes into the storehouse, God will prosper you spiritually and materially."[1]

I have found this to be true. Whenever I've taken a church position, I've never asked about the salary before agreeing to come. I've trusted God with my pay and He has always been faithful. Some churches have been generous, others have not, but God has always provided. If we first give ourselves, God knows how to provide for those who take their stewardship seriously.

> *We think getting is the answer to all our problems, but in God's economy giving is the answer.*

Our world system is backwards. We've become convinced that winning the lottery or gambling will make us rich, successful and happy. Read the stories of those who have bought into this myth. People lie to them, steal from them, and often they are unhappy in the long run. Many end up bankrupt. Why? They don't understand God's plan of economy. We think *getting* is the answer to all our problems, but in God's economy *giving* is the answer. Through our giving we understand that Christ supplies all our needs according to His riches in glory in Christ Jesus.

In his Gospel, Matthew gave us a clear warning and an eternal principle:

> Do not store up for yourselves treasures on earth, where moth and rust destroy, and where thieves break in and steal. But store up for yourselves treasures in heaven, where neither moth nor rust destroys, and where thieves do not break in or steal; for where your treasure is, there your heart will be also. (6:19–21)

My friend Bill Stafford, an evangelist and revivalist, wrote an excellent book on Spirit-filled giving. He provides great insight into the passage regarding the Macedonians:

> These verses are the steps to a life of glorious liberty beyond all human understanding. Until a person is brought to this truth and starts to release his hold on things, there will always be an area of fear in his life that the Devil can use to suppress victorious living. Every area of our lives must be opened and surrendered unreservedly to the lordship of Christ, or the Enemy will attack and overcome us.
>
> Because of incorrect doctrine, traditional preaching, or half-truth, we have wandered in the wilderness of doing the best we can. If you own ninety-nine acres of ground but another person owns an acre right in the middle of your ninety-nine, he must be given a right of way to his one acre. This means he can walk all over your territory to get to his. So it is in the life of the Christian. That one acre you fail to give becomes a stronghold for Satan, and he will walk all over your surrendered territory to get to his one acre.[2]

Coveting Results in Loss

Finances are the root of some of the biggest problems in the home. Looking at finances from an unbiblical perspective results in bondage and debt that will cost more than we can imagine. Because of our own greed as parents, we are raising a materialistic, "I want it now" generation. As a result of coveting, we are not fulfilling the Great Commission and supporting missions as we should.

Look at the Macedonians. They didn't give out of their riches, they gave out of their poverty. We deceive ourselves if we pray, "Lord bless those who give and those who can't afford to give." God blesses to the extent we allow Him to through our obedience. When we invest in things that matter to God, we are investing in things that will last for eternity. Generosity is not the exclusive territory of those who have great wealth. In fact, it is not measured by quantity but by sacrifice. It's not about equal gifts; it's about equal sacrifice.

Every Sunday there are those who leave church as soon as the preacher says "Amen." Many fail to worship and honor God with their lips and gifts. In reality, they sacrifice their lives, their families and their testimony on the frivolous and temporal.

Don't worry. God doesn't need our money. He wants our lives. Remember, stewardship is lordship. Corinth abounded in every gift, but they hadn't passed the giving test. We pass or fail the test of giving based on how convinced we are that our lives belong to Christ.

In the Macedonians' example and Paul's instructions to the Corinthians, we find a formula for giving. Instead of trying to "nickel and dime" God or arguing with Him about tithing off the gross or the net, Paul tells us clearly, "Now concerning the collection for the saints, as I directed the churches of Galatia, so do you also. On the first day of every week each one of you is to put aside and save, as he may prosper, so that no collections be made when I come" (1 Cor. 16:1–2).

We are to give first of ourselves. The Scripture further instructs us to give methodically ("on the first day of the week"), personally ("each one of you"), regularly ("put aside and save") and according to our ability ("as he may prosper").

Those of us who have been blessed by God's grace and goodness need to fireproof our finances, our motives and our priorities through giving. Jesus came full of grace and truth. We have received His fullness and grace upon grace. In light of that, think about your giving. God's grace is free, full and functioning. Does your giving reflect His goodness in your life?

The Macedonians were at the bottom of the economic ladder, but at the top of the giving ladder. They were living examples of what grace should do to us. They viewed their giving as an act of worship and obedience. In extreme poverty they exhibited rich generosity, showing overflowing joy even in difficult circumstances.

Many believers have no vision for missions and ministry because they are walking around in a fog of selfishness. Our resources don't go as far as they should because we're covetous and materialistic. Remember Achan in Joshua 7? He stole what belonged to the Lord, and it cost him and his entire family their lives. He said, "I saw," "I coveted" and "I took." That's a danger in our media-driven society. We see stuff, we want it and we take it, even if it means disobeying God. After all, we've worked hard, we've earned it—it's ours, right?

"For the love of money is a root of all sorts of evil, and some by longing for it have wandered away from the faith and pierced themselves with many griefs" (1 Tim. 6:10). Warren Wiersbe says Paul shared four facts with Timothy to warn us about the dangers of covetousness:

1. Wealth does not bring contentment (v. 6). The word contentment means "an inner sufficiency that keeps us at peace in spite of outward circumstances." True content-

ment comes from godliness in the heart, not wealth in the hand.

2. Wealth is not lasting (v. 7). Whatever wealth we amass goes to the government, our heirs and perhaps charity and the church. We all know the answer to the question, "How much did he leave?" Everything!

3. Our basic needs are easily met (v. 8). Food, clothing and shelter are basic needs. If we lose them, we lose the ability to secure other things. Henry David Thoreau, the naturalist of the 1800s, reminded us that a man is wealthy in proportion to the number of things he can afford to do without.

4. The desire for wealth leads to sin (vv. 9–10). "They that will be rich," is the accurate translation. It describes a person who must have more and more material things in order to be happy and feel successful. But riches are a trap, and they lead to bondage, not freedom. Instead of giving satisfaction, riches create additional desires, and these must be satisfied.[3]

In my early days at Sherwood, Jonathan Beasley was our youth minister. To keep himself from making an impulsive purchase, he kept his credit card frozen in ice in his freezer. If he went shopping and found something he thought he "had to have," he would go home and let the card thaw out. If he still "needed" it after going home and thinking about it, he could go back for it. Some of us need to freeze our spending so we can liberate our giving.

Some of us need to freeze our spending so we can liberate our giving.

Beyond the Tithe

If the Macedonians could give out of their poverty, why don't we give out of our prosperity? Some have tithed for years, but never give a penny more than ten percent. They miss out on the joy of giving. They obey the law, but perhaps they haven't bought into grace. Giving as unto the Lord in light of grace moves us beyond percentage. It makes us want to give our life, our love, our all.

I can testify today that God meets our needs when we learn to be generous. If we give when we can't afford it and when we can, God makes ends meet. I don't know how He does it, but I can testify that He does. When you reckon on God for your sufficiency, something happens that cannot be explained.

Through the years my wife and I have sought to understand that the tithe is holy unto the Lord as Malachi says. We've also endeavored to give the tithe and then some. We can't out-give God.

Years ago I heard a preacher talk on giving, and it revolutionized my understanding of stewardship. He said, "Since the garden of Eden, God has set aside something for Himself as a reminder to man that everything is the Lord's." Then he nailed me with a biblical truth I can't get over: "God always reserves something for Himself in the physical realm, where man obtains his living, to remind man that God is the owner of everything. God reserved for Himself a tree, a day, a city, the tithe, a year when the land was to stand idle." The facts here are clear. What God sets aside as holy, as His, is a reminder that we are stewards, not owners. Keeping what belongs to God opens the door for moths and rust to destroy all we have.

One of my friends and heroes, John Bisagno, wrote the following:

> Have you ever needed money and prayed to God to give it to you? Have you, then, had that prayer answered? Where do you think that money came from? Did God print up money in heaven and send it down by an angel? No. He touched someone's heart and led them to give you that money.
>
> What right does God have to do that? The right of ownership! If all the silver and gold is God's, He has the right to redistribute His wealth. When you ask God to give you money, you are acknowledging God's property rights, God's ownership. But, when you fail to tithe, you deny that right. Therefore, if you do not tithe, you have absolutely no right to ask God to give you money to meet your financial needs. In such an act, you are asking God to do something in prayer which, by your action, you deny He has the right to do. The non-tither has no right to come to the church and ask for money for car payments, utilities or food. And the church has no obligation to give it. I have no right to ask God to do something in prayer which I deny in practice He has the right to do.[4]

Let's close with several principles we need to fireproof our finances:

- When we have experienced grace, we should express our gratitude to God through giving.
- When Jesus is Lord, it is reflected in our giving and spending.
- When the heart is right, giving to the Lord and His work is never a burden.

- To do the work of God, we must see the need of investing in Kingdom business. It's not the responsibility of the few to provide for the many. Are you carrying your share of the load?
- Giving is as much a part of worship as prayer, preaching and singing. We should be as enthusiastic about the offering as we are about our favorite song or choir special.
- Never forget the law of the harvest: You reap what you sow, you reap more than you sow and you reap later than you sow. I can't ask God to help me in the realm of my finances if I'm not honoring Him in that area.
- God loves a cheerful giver. Cheer up! What you send ahead is earning interest.

The tremendous height of these proud trees invites opposition from another enemy. They bear scars from hundreds of lightning strikes as signs of their battle for survival. But not even the most powerful strikes on the most vulnerable areas of the tree can kill a sequoia. It may take years to overcome the assault, but the tree will survive, heal and remain unshaken and stalwart.

Beloved, do not be surprised at the fiery ordeal among you, which comes upon you for your testing, as though some strange thing were happening to you.
(1 Pet. 4:12)

9

Fireproof for Times of Conflict and Crisis

YOU PROBABLY wouldn't be reading this book if you hadn't been burned at some point. Everyone has hills and valleys. Everyone goes through the fire of adversity, when shallow comforts fall flat. What we need in times of crisis is not pop psychology or peppy preaching. We need power to sustain us. We need to see our way clear through the smoke.

People talk about the "good old days" when life seemed simpler. Maybe it was. Regardless, we don't live there any more. Life is complex, confusing and complicated. When I was growing up, ice cream came in three flavors: vanilla, chocolate and strawberry. Now we have hundreds of flavors and can mix in anything we want, from gummy bears to cookies. The choices are overwhelming.

How does our society deal with the complex crises of life? Sometimes by sticking its head in the sand. Years ago on the CBS Evening News, Charles Osgood reported on a mall that had banned baseball caps from being worn backwards because they saw it as a gang symbol. "This proves," he said, "that when faced with a serious problem, we will do any- thing to keep from dealing with the real issue." Some wal- low in problems while others live in denial, but few take hold of a crisis and transform it into something useful.

If we don't learn from the crises of life, we're doomed to repeat our mistakes over and over. To rise above, we must learn that the fire is for our refining, so the gold can shine through in gleaming purity.

> *To rise above, we must learn that the fire is for our refining, so the gold can shine through in gleaming purity.*

Although we know crises will come, we often don't pre- pare for them. People put off getting car or health insurance, hoping something doesn't hap- pen—and when it does, it's a crisis and often a catastrophe.

While doing a study with our staff on how leaders deal with crises, I jotted down these words about the great In- dian chief, Sitting Bull:

> The Sioux had learned to live with crisis through centu- ries of living with the dangers of their ever-changing envi- ronment. A product of his culture, Sitting Bull remained acutely aware of the dangers that lack of preparation could engender and he kept himself closely attuned to all the ele- ments of his environment that could suddenly change and plunge him into a life-threatening situation. He had a plan B for every possibility.
>
> Custer too had experienced crisis during the Civil War, but he was too star-struck by the opportunity to shine in battle to consider the real possibility of crisis threatening his campaign with the Sioux. He had so long led the charmed

life of a commander who could do no wrong that he assumed his confrontation with the Enemy would go according to plan. He thought the campaign would bring him into the White House and the Presidency. His mind was at the White House, Sitting Bull's was on the battlefield.[1]

The punch that knocks us out is not the hardest one; it's the one we don't expect.

Our Response: The Real Issue

Some people fall into the pit of failure when crisis comes. Some shrug their shoulders and go into survival mode. The person who wants to grow in the conflict seeks to learn from it.

As a pastor, I've watched all kinds of responses to crisis:

"Trouble happens."

"This really isn't happening; I'm just having a nightmare."

"This has happened before, and it always happens to me."

"It must be God's will." (Often used as a cop-out for not dealing with it.)

"If it's trouble, I deserve it."

"I must have bad karma."

In reality, the issue is not the crisis itself, but how we respond to it.

We need to understand that life has difficult bumps in the road. Once I accept that life is not a fairy tale, crises become less difficult to handle. We are wrong to assume life should be easy. The world is sinful and fallen, and we are in a battle. As Paul Harvey said in a broadcast, "In times like these it is good to remember there have always been times like these." Some of us are so prone to being burned by the sparks of life that we bemoan the slightest conflict as if no one had ever faced such difficulties. The truth is that somewhere, someone is facing a more serious and difficult crisis than we are.

When faced with a crisis, the questions to ask are not "Why me?" or "Why this?" or "Why now?" In reality the only honest question is: "What now?" You and I aren't the first to see the sparks of adversity turn into a flaming fire all around us—and we won't be the last.

My parents, with others of their generation, lived through events I can't even begin to imagine: the stock market crash of 1929 and the Great Depression, World War II with its resulting food and gas rationing, the Korean conflict, the Cuban Missile Crisis and much more.

My parents' generation did not have easy lives. My dad was days away from his Army discharge when World War II broke out. He served his country until the end of the war. He was assigned to the 509th Bombardment Group in the South Pacific, which was responsible for dropping the first atomic bomb.

During his stateside preparation he was able to be with my mom, and soon they were expecting their first child. After a difficult pregnancy, my mother lost the baby at birth, and nearly died herself. Dad was given a special leave of absence to stay with her. Because of shortages and rationing, her family had to sacrifice to provide for her recovery.

As a teenager I watched my dad suffer the death of a dream. He was a pharmacist and had always dreamed of owning his own store. For twelve long years he worked to make that dream a reality. He eked out a living and destroyed his health, never taking a vacation during those years. He was forced to close when he could no longer compete with the growing drug store chains.

At the same time my mom developed breast cancer. She went to sleep expecting a routine surgery and woke up to find they had done a double mastectomy. It was devastating to her self-image, and in those days there was no cosmetic surgery to repair the damage. But she learned to use her crisis as an opportunity to minister to others. Why? She had been there and survived the fire.

Over the last thirty years of her life, she had constant health problems. The week before she died she went into a diabetic coma and didn't recover. We were never able to say goodbye.

I watched my dad grieve for the rest of his life. He visited her grave every day. He would take his shovel, some sand and weed killer to make sure the gravesite was neat and clean. Those last few years were hard. His heart was weak, and he and I decided to make the "do not resuscitate" decision should it be needed. A few years after our initial discussion, he had another procedure on his heart. The hospital records had failed to note the "do not resuscitate" request, and I had to discuss it with him again, as if once wasn't hard enough. During his last stay in the hospital, I knew he wouldn't make it out. Terri and I watched him pass away, delirious, panicked and gasping for breath.

Terri's dad served in Korea and was a POW for over two years. He nearly died in the prison camp. In fact, he was thrown in the "death house" with dead and dying men for over three weeks. He rarely talked about the trauma of those days. In his later years he had multiple strokes and was diagnosed with post traumatic stress disorder. Little had we realized how much those years in the hellish prison camp had affected him.

The last three years of his life, he was in a Veteran's Administration nursing home. We were saddened when we visited because we remembered his vibrance and strength.

As I think about all our parents lived through, the "good old days" don't seem that good. But rarely did I hear them discuss those times, much less complain about them. The problem with some of us is we think nobody knows the trouble we've seen. We can honestly deceive ourselves into thinking our trivial disappointments are crises worthy of tears and travail.

We Need Each Other

One truth I learned while filming *Fireproof* is that a fireman never leaves his partner behind, especially in a fire. That's why it grieves me to see once-active believers who have bailed out because of a crisis. Rather than running to God, they ran away from Him and His church—the very thing they needed in their trial.

If we don't learn from those more experienced than us, we forfeit the value of their example and advice.

In the crisis moments of life, we need people who have been through the fire before—seasoned veterans. We may be rookies at fighting this crisis, but we can find others who have survived the battle. If we don't learn from those more experienced than we are, we forfeit the value of their example and advice.

I've been blessed by the godly counsel of older men all my life. It seems that God has often given me favor with ministry leaders ten to twenty years my senior. They are seasoned saints whose counsel has saved me numerous times. When going through a crisis, I seek their counsel, wisdom and insight. I've learned to listen and, hopefully, apply what I've learned. Their advice has spared me much heartache.

In a crisis find older Christians who have walked the road of adversity. Seek their counsel, consider their judgment and learn from them. If you are older obey the Scriptures by investing in young believers. They need your wisdom. Seek them out; don't wait for them to find you. It's amazing what you can learn from one another over a cup of coffee or a sandwich.

One of the things that the experience of older believers will give you is a long-term perspective, one that leads you to make decisions based on principle rather than expediency. My Christian parents, for example, taught me to always do the right thing—keep your word, maintain your character and do what's right, even if it hurts. I have found that this policy works best because the decisions you make don't come back to haunt you.

One example from the business world of doing the right thing is the "Tylenol Crisis." When evidence surfaced in 1982 that someone had tampered with Tylenol®, Johnson & Johnson took every bottle off the shelves; it cost them over $100 million. But when the crisis was over, 93% of Americans said the company did the right thing and they would buy the product again.

Dealing with a Crisis

Another thing that overwhelms us in times of conflict is trying to fight too many fires at once. We run here and there, throwing water on scattered fires, but never dealing with any of them completely. Often a crisis will recur because we've dealt with the symptoms, not the problem.

I once read the following statement: "Never try to solve all the problems all at once—make them line up for you one by one. Whether you face three problems, thirty or three hundred . . . make them stand in single file so you can face only one at a time." This is a key to emotional balance. If your emotions run your life, you just might sell your birthright for a bowl of soup.

John Mason, in his book *Why Ask Why? If You Know the Right Questions You Can Find the Right Answers*, poses this question: "Is the only time you do any deep praying when you find yourself in a hole?" He goes on to admonish us regarding the most important aspect of crisis management:

If God is your Father, please call home. Corrie ten Boom said, "The Devil smiles when we make plans. He laughs when we get too busy. But he trembles when we pray." When you feel swept off your feet, it's time to go back on your knees.

"Time spent in communion with God is never lost," says Gordon Lindsay. The highest purpose of faith or prayer is not to change your circumstances but to change you. Pray to do the will of God in every situation; nothing else is worth praying for.

James Hudson Taylor put it this way: "Do not have your concert and tune your instruments afterwards. Begin the day with God." Martin Luther once said, "I have so much to do today that I shall spend the first three hours in prayer." Prayer may not change all things for you, but it sure changes you for all things. He's waiting to hear from you.[2]

If you are going through a crisis, remember this: God's ear is open to our earnest cries. Draw near to God. Get so near to Him you can hear Him whisper in your heart. When we seek Him, we will find Him.

Good can come out of the crises of life. During the Great Chicago Fire of 1871, nearly everything D.L. Moody had built was destroyed, including his church and home. Before it was contained, the fire destroyed 1,800 buildings; property damage was estimated at over $200 million. Ninety thousand were left homeless and three hundred died.

> *If you are going through a crisis, remember this: God's ear is open to our earnest cries.*

God turned the tragedy of the fire into an opportunity. Moody immediately began raising money to rebuild his investment. In less than three months, the Northside Tabernacle was constructed to accommodate the work temporarily. It became a hub for the ministry of the gospel to the community. Later the Chicago Avenue Church replaced the tabernacle.

On the night of the fire, Moody was preaching about the life of Christ. He asked the packed house, "What will you do with Jesus Christ?" Rather than giving an invitation to respond, Moody told the people to go home to think about the question. Moody never saw that same audience again. He said, "It was the worst mistake I ever made."

Moody's biography records the critical decision he made as a result of the fire: "I tell you of one lesson I learned that night . . . that is, when I preach, I press Christ upon the people then and there and try to bring them to a decision on the spot."[3]

Before the tragic fire Moody was immersed in secondary matters of administration, which drained him of the time needed to fulfill his calling. But God prepared him for what was coming. Three days before the devastating fire, Moody wept and prayed and cried out to God for greater power and service in ministry. He prayed for the fullness of the Spirit in his life and ministry. The fire cast Moody on the mercy and grace of God.

From that great crisis was birthed a single-focused desire for evangelism, greater power in his preaching and a greater harvest of souls. In 1873 Moody preached his first evangelistic campaign in Great Britain and stayed there for two years. When he preached at Charlotte's Chapel in Edinburgh, Scotland, 3,000 came to Christ. For the next fourteen years, the church baptized 1,000 people a year.

One Anglican pastor says, "Moody took the people of Britain in one hand, and America in another, and lifted them up to the glory of God." God took the setbacks and suffering of the fire and turned it into an opportunity for greater ministry.[4]

What setback in your life could be turned into a platform for ministry? What trial could open up a new dimension of truth? What failure could result in your seeking God in a greater way and walking by faith like never before? In the midst of crisis, it pays to seek Christ.

Here are some suggestions on how to build this into your life:

1. Acknowledge that conflicts are a part of life. Where there is movement, there is friction.
2. Thank God for the conflict. Yes, you read that correctly. Anything that causes you to seek the Lord is a blessing.
3. Seek restoration and reconciliation if at all possible. Write a letter. Make a phone call. Ask for an appointment. Secret sin requires secret confession; public sin requires public confession. Make reconciliation on the level necessary. Remember, you are not responsible for how others act or react, but only for yourself.
4. Don't point fingers. Look in the mirror of your own heart. Is there a flaw, a log in your eye that God is trying to speak to you about? Is this an ongoing problem? If so, you may need to seek wisdom from a Christian counselor.
5. Don't run from conflict and crisis. In every battle there is a blessing. Remember, Joseph said, "You meant it for evil, but God meant it for good."
6. Don't be in denial about conflict. Many of us shut down when there is a conflict. We withdraw, quit talking and start building walls. The right response is to seek the Lord and prayerfully address the situation.
7. Leave the results to God. When we have taken our stand on His Word, we can rest knowing He will respond as He has promised.

The great sequoias are not deformed by harsh weather; the strongest, most direct winds actually serve to strengthen the trees rather than weaken them. Each blast of wind creates tiny fractures in the bark which produce a more pliable and resilient tree, able to bend but not break.

Each man's work will become evident;
for the day will show it because it is
to be revealed with fire, and the
fire itself will test the quality
of each man's work.
(1 Cor. 3:13)

10

Fireproof Your Life for Eternity

THESE PAGES contain a great deal about fireproofing our lives. As we've read, having a fireproof life does not mean we will avoid the fire. It means we've made preparations for the fiery trials that will inevitably come.

Computer firewalls accomplish this very purpose. Because we know inappropriate material can come into our homes via the Internet, we set up firewalls and filters to block a host of destructive content. The Internet connection travels into your computer through multiple ports, and a firewall allows you to turn ports "on" and "off" to control the traffic into your home or business. Without a firewall, you expose yourself and others to the flames.

Ultimately, for the believer and non-believer, there will be a fire. The unbeliever will be cast into the everlasting flames. The believer's fire is of a different nature: Our works will be tried "as by fire," according to Paul's instructions to the Corinthians.

Paul wrote, "For we must all appear before the judgment seat of Christ, so that each one may be recompensed for his deeds in the body, according to what he has done, whether good or bad" (2 Cor. 5:10). This verse compares the judgment of believers to the Greek Olympic games, where the ruler, governor or judge sat on a "bema"—a raised platform—

Have you made the necessary preparations to stand before the judgment seat of Christ?

to address the crowd, grant awards or render a verdict. It was the place where a case was heard and a ruling rendered by one in authority. No bribes or grading on a curve. We will stand alone before the Magistrate of glory to hear His verdict—not on our salvation, of course, but on our service and works as believers.

Preparing for Eternity

How can we pass the ultimate fire test? What do we need to learn in this life that will prepare us for this test in the next? Have you paused to think about areas of vulnerability? Are you aware of the schemes of the Devil? Have you made the necessary preparations to stand before the judgment seat of Christ?

Caleb's father talks to him about unconditional love and everlasting life through Christ.

Whether we realize it or not, we are one breath, one heart-beat away from a determined state of rewards, whether it be joy or embarrassment. Where we end in time, we start again in eternity. There are no second runs at life; this isn't a dress rehearsal. We live, then die, then live again for eternity. There are no chances for improvement on the other side. What-ever rewards or treasures we have there are determined on this side.

Are you living now what you want to be then? Or are you living in procrastination, thinking you've got all the time in the world to get your act together? Can you really afford to neglect that area where your testimony is vulnerable, if not questionable?

We must realize this life is preparation for eternity. The judgment seat of Christ will be a day of accounting when all Christians must appear. Not a few. Not just the preachers. All who have called on the name of Christ for salvation. We must ask ourselves, *What am I doing in this life to prepare for the judgment seat of Christ? Am I being a good steward, cooper-ating with the Savior in my sanctification?*

On that day of judgment, our works will be judged in light of eternity. Our true motives will be revealed and our true character will be examined. Paul said each man's work will be "revealed with fire" (1 Cor. 3:13). Anything selfish, egocentric or petty will burn up. The fire will test "the qual-ity of each man's work"—not the size, but the sort. In Ro-mans 14:12 we read, "So then, each one of us will give an account of himself to God."

The emphasis is on motives, not achievements. Many impressive résumés will burn up on that day. Titles and de-grees will go by the wayside. Only that which brings honor and glory to Jesus Christ will survive.

Look back at Paul's phrase: "whether good or bad." Those words should stop us in our tracks. The words "good or bad" do not mean "morally good or evil"; they refer to worth or value. Are my works worthy in light of eternity? Paul describes six kinds of building materials—three are cheap and three are of great value. The reason many people ruin their testimony and lose their witness is because they've built their lives with flammable materials. Wood, hay and stubble will go up in smoke, but the gold, silver and precious stone will withstand the flames.

While we are not saved by works, we *are* rewarded for them—and that's good news! We were created in Christ Jesus to do good works. Our works don't get us to heaven but they follow us there. Here's the reality: Everyone won't get the same thing in heaven. God's not out to be fair, but just.

I have several friends who started out in ministry but are no longer serving. Some failed because of pornography—they didn't guard their minds. Some lost their marriages—they didn't guard their hearts.

I have one friend who lost his ministry over habitual lying. He would lie for no apparent reason and did it so often he became unaware of it. Another friend has an anger problem. He reacts and overreacts in ways that make him unapproachable. Many of us, like them, have limited what God can do in our lives. One day we will stand before the judgment seat of Christ. Some of us will be saved "as by fire." I'm not the judge, but I do know there are steps we must take if we are going to finish well.

Our Desperate Need: Life in the Spirit

While I want to do all I can to live a fireproof life, I also want to do all I can to keep a different kind of fire burning—the fire in my heart. I want to be like the two on the road to Emmaus: "Did not our hearts burn within us?" I want to have a burning heart for God. I want to finish well and not blow it at the end. I've spent too much time and energy to give up or cave in now, but the temptation is always there. The issues addressed in this book are real. They are common areas where the battle rages—traps that have captured and wounded many believers along the journey.

The lives of Noah, Moses, the prophets, apostles and every martyr in Christian history show us that storms assail the godly. A fireproof life means we can survive the test and live as overcomers even in the toughest times.

We will not overcome, however, if having begun in the Spirit, we live in the flesh. While we all believe there is nothing we can do to save ourselves, we have a hard time grasping Christ's teaching about our continued growth: "Apart from Me you can do nothing" (John 15:5). In effect we are burned when we fail to depend on the Holy Spirit.

I heard a story about a Christian school class that quoted the Apostles' Creed every morning. Each student was to quote their assigned portion of the creed, which includes the line "I believe in the Holy Spirit . . . ." One morning as they recited the creed line by line, there was a sudden silence. After a pause, a boy in the back of the room spoke up and said, "The boy who believes in the Holy Spirit is not here this morning."

Unfortunately that's what has happened in many of our

churches—those who believe in the Holy Spirit are missing! We fail to pray and prepare ourselves because we don't understand our desperate need for the Holy Spirit.

When you study the genesis and genius of Christianity, one thing stands out: God's ways are not our ways, and His thoughts are not our thoughts. The way He reveals Himself may not be how we would choose. He contradicts our complex formulas and calls us to simple faith, bypassing programs and looking for praying people. He calls us to a narrow road.

There is great danger today in trying to do the work of the Spirit in the energy of the flesh. Lacking power, we buy a generator. Lacking fire, we strike a match. Lacking living water, we buy bottled water. When Paul went to Corinth, he was in the center of the world's collected wisdom; the gospel was considered foolish. But Paul was willing to be called a fool for the sake of Christ. Today, however, we are guilty of a different kind of foolishness: We seek to perfect ourselves in the flesh, and the credibility of the gospel is smeared.

God contradicts our complex formulas and calls us to simple faith, bypassing programs and looking for praying people.

We'll never live a fireproof life if we are consumed with pleasing this present age. There has never been a culture since the dawn of the church in which a Christian could feel "at home." Unfortunately, though, some hope for heaven while acting as much like the world as possible.

We are to be in the world, but not of it. We were saved out of the world to take the gospel back into the world and bring others out of the world—and the cycle continues. We are pilgrims, strangers, exiles and aliens. We're on a journey. We should pray for God's keeping power until we reach our destination.

With today's emphases on success, relevance to the culture and seeker-friendliness, we are in danger of living empty lives. We work hard to relate to the world, and in the end we are not real. This is a sad imitation of the real thing. And when any pressure comes, we cave in. As Ron Dunn put it, "We are not the stuff of which martyrs are made."

Not long ago I was speaking at a conference where a remarkable singer from Wales shared about the Welsh revival of 1904. The fire and glory fell there, and 100,000 were converted in six months. Jails were closed and prayer meetings covered the landscape. Newspapers printed the names of converts in each city and village. As I sat there longing to see that kind of work happen again, I realized that about twenty percent of the crowd had slipped out to watch a college football championship on television. God will never send a movement of His Spirit to a people who care more about football than His glory.

Before the awakening at the time of the Wesley brothers, Christianity was at a low point. The Puritans had been buried and the Methodists hadn't been born. It was a spiritually dark time. But the turning of the tide occurs at lowest ebb. John Wesley preached with power, Charles wrote anointed songs and God worked. England was likely saved from civil war because of this move of God.

Today we lack that kind of power. We often shrivel up at the first sign of testing and trials. We shrink back when the world confronts us and demands our authenticity. The highway is littered with fallen ministers, compromised churches, tainted ministries and other embarrassing examples. There's an old poem that reads, "How sad will be the days in store, When voice and vision come no more." These days are increasingly upon us.

Many churches could change their name to First Church of Laodicea. We're lukewarm. Consider Jesus' words in Revelation 3:16: "So because you are lukewarm, and neither hot nor cold, I will spit you out of my mouth." The root of lukewarmness is apathy and comfort. Could your church withstand a time of testing? David Kingdon wrote, "Only in the hot furnace of affliction do we as Christians let go of the dross to which, in our foolishness, we ardently cling."[1]

Home Before Dark

Vance Havner went through a dark time in his early years. He was the boy preacher who started his ministry at twelve years of age. As he got older, Havner started reading liberal theology. Trying to relate to the world, he grew discouraged. He returned home to help his mother run the family grocery store. One night they were robbed and the store was burned down.

In his classic sermon "Home Before Dark," Havner shared about the experience:

God spoke to me and told me, "If you'll get some of those new notions out of your head and go back and preach what you preached when you were a boy, I'll make a way for you." So I got out of the novelty shop and got back in the antique shop. God started opening doors. He gave me a new message and a new mission. Then God put me through a test. For two years I couldn't sleep at night, and I suffered from nervous exhaustion. Then God called me to begin my preaching ministry. No doctor would have told me to go into that kind of work—sleeping in a different bed every week when I couldn't sleep in any bed. I yielded to the Lord and said, "Lord, I'm going to make the venture, and if I'm wrong stop me."[2]

Havner went to Grand Rapids to preach at Mel Trotter's mission and then to Moody Bible Institute. There he came down with a severe case of the flu. The Devil taunted him saying, "Now what are you going to do?" He was alone and without clear plans, but God had not forgotten him.

Another severe test Havner faced was the death of his wife Sara after thirty-three years of marriage. Sara died at 2:15 on a Sunday morning, and Havner preached at 11:00 that

> *We won't be able to stand and sing to the Lord until we lay ourselves on the altar.*

day in their home church in Greensboro. During the dark days that followed, he wrote his most popular book *Though I Walk Through the Valley.*

He wrote, "Lord, I don't understand it. I thought we'd have a sweet old age together, and here I'm left like I started; but You know what You're doing." Out of that dark valley of trial and testing came a new dimension to his ministry. The brokenhearted sought Havner out, and his ministry blossomed even more in his latter years.

How do we stay on track in the midst of hardship and testing? "When the burnt offering began, the song to the LORD also began" (2 Chron. 29:27). We won't be able to stand and sing to the Lord until we lay ourselves on the altar. We offer the sacrifices of penitence (Ps. 51:17), of person (Rom. 12:1–2) and of praise (Heb. 13:15). That's the divine order.

We're facing a demonized world, and the only way to overcome is with a demonstration of the Spirit of God in power. The Good News has been defended and declared, but what it needs most is to be demonstrated. The best argument for Christianity is a life that reflects Christ in every sense of the word.

Havner often told stories of growing up in the foothills of the Blue Ridge Mountains outside Hickory, North Carolina. As a boy, he knew that no matter where he went, he was supposed to be home by sundown—it was non-negotiable. Later in life Havner said, "I find myself praying, 'Lord, I want to get home before dark, before I lose my faculties.'" Dr. William Culbertson used to say, "Lord, when Thou seest that my work is done, let me not linger with failing powers . . . a workless worker in a world of work."

Havner wrote:

> I'd like to get home before dark because although you're saved, you're never safe as far as your testimony's concerned until you get home. They will all remember the big blunder you made on the last mile of the way and forget all the good things you did all the way back up the road.[3]

Think about it. It's not hard to think of the name of some athlete, politician, preacher or evangelist who was once used of God but blew it somewhere along the road. They had so much in their favor but they fell morally or ethically. Now when you hear their name all you think about is their failure. The good has been snuffed out by their poor decisions.

Psalm 71:18 says, "And even when I am old and gray, O God, do not forsake me until I declare Your strength to this generation, Your power to all who are to come." As we get older we may feel life has passed us by or we've failed along the way and God can't use us anymore. Don't give up the battle. Don't quit until you hear God calling you home.

Some consider afflictions to be a training class in the school of faith. Others, because they have not guarded their hearts and minds in Christ Jesus, see their troubles as reminders of failure. But afflictions, tests and trials are often God's blessings in disguise. Our crosses can be ladders that lead us to a higher level spiritually.

As gold is tried and refined by fire, so the fires of adversity reveal the sincerity of our faith. Many of us can testify that the fire burned away dross, enabling us to enter a new dimension in our spiritual lives. As the hammer forges the steel, so the tests of life forge our faith. There can be no triumphs without a trial.

We have a long way to go on our journey. We don't need any more casualties. We need men and women who can stand in the storms of life—fireproof believers who will arrive at the gates of heaven with their testimony intact. Let it be our prayer that we all get home before dark.

Do you not know that those who run in a race all run, but only one receives the prize? Run in such a way that you may win. Everyone who competes in the games exercises self-control in all things. They then do it to receive a perishable wreath, but we an imperishable. Therefore I run in such a way, as not without aim; I box in such a way, as not beating the air; but I discipline my body and make it my slave, so that, after I have preached to others, I myself will not be disqualified. (1 Cor. 9:24-27)

Therefore, since we have so great a cloud of witnesses surrounding us, let us also lay aside every encumbrance and the sin which so easily entangles us, and let us run with endurance the race that is set before us, fixing our eyes on Jesus, the author and perfecter of faith. (Heb. 12:1–2)

*Fires in sequoia forests actually produce favorable results:
when the cone of the sequoia is burned, it dries out, pops
open and disperses its seeds. One tree can produce tens of
thousands of seeds. The key to the growth of the seeds is its
nitrogen-rich soil, the result of layer upon layer of ash from
many fires. And so life springs from death and the flames
result in new birth.*

Epilogue:

Leaving a Legacy

IN THE FIRST chapter I used the sequoia as a metaphor for a fireproof life. I was inspired to do so after looking at photographs of the trees taken by my friend Ken Jenkins, and hearing all he had discovered about these giants of the forest. I was especially struck by a fascinating fact he learned from a local forestry expert.

While Ken and the forester were talking, a massive sequoia fell, landing with a thundering force that shook the ground. The forester explained that the giant tree did not fall because of the hundreds of past fires that had attacked it over the course of its long life. The tree had simply reached the full extent of its life. But even in death, the tree has a life-giving function: to expose fertile soil and provide nutrients to other plants and animals, enabling them to survive and even thrive as a result of the tree's long-standing faithfulness to its call.

In the same way, believers who have lived their lives to the glory of God continue to bear fruit even in death. Their lives make an impact that still resonates in the forest of the faithful. We are blessed by those who have gone before us—those whose lives challenge us to be holy and to know Christ more fully.

Two of my dearest friends and greatest heroes are Ron Dunn and Vance Havner, both of whom are in glory now. When I'm going through the fire, I often think of them and wish I had their counsel.

But though dead, their lives still speak. Ron was a pastor and Bible teacher and the greatest expositor I ever heard. His insights into Scripture have deeply impacted my under-standing of God's Word. Ron suffered deeply. His oldest son took his life in the 1970s, and Ron's book *When Heaven is Silent* deals with his struggles following that tragedy. Ron also battled several medical issues most of his life. Out of his weakness and the fires of adversity, God used him to teach thousands how to fireproof their lives.

Vance Havner was a twentieth-century prophet. Even without a college education, he wrote thirty-nine books. He was a wordsmith who could say more in one sentence than most preachers can say in a thirty-minute sermon. Dr. Havner went through a time of doubt early in his ministry. He expe-rienced deep physical suffering in the 1960s as well as the death of his wife from a devastating disease. His book *Though I Walk through the Valley* is a classic. He didn't wallow in the valleys of life, but learned from his trials and used those les-sons to teach others also.[1]

I refer to these giants in my life repeatedly in my books and sermons. One of our staff members says you can't be a member of Sherwood for two weeks without hearing me quote one of them. Although Vance died in 1986 and Ron in 2001, the investment they made in the soil of my heart lives on. They planted something in me that I'll never get over as long as God gives me breath. Hopefully when I'm gone my life will affect others in the same way. We should all pray that it would be so.

Paul said to young Timothy, "You therefore, my son, be strong in the grace that is in Christ Jesus. The things which you have heard from me in the presence of many witnesses, entrust these to faithful men who will be able to teach others also" (2 Tim. 2:1–2).

When Paul says "be strong," he uses a passive verb. It means that Timothy should look to the Lord, not himself, for the strength needed to live up to the demands of his calling. Our strength is in the Lord. When times of testing come, when the fires rage around us, we need to know we cannot and will not be able to stand on our own. We stand firm in the Lord alone.

As I look across the landscape of faith, I see giants who have roamed the land. Like the mighty sequoia trees, they have given us shade in which to find rest. They have spoken words that have comforted our souls in times of trouble. They have stood for truth and righteousness in the face of opposition and persecution. We know what we know today because they lived a full and meaningful life. Although they are gone they continue to nourish us and serve as examples for us.

Each of us has been entrusted with a great spiritual heritage. The giants of the past may have fallen, but they have left their sermons, books, messages and wisdom as an investment in the soil of our hearts.

William Barclay writes, "The teacher is a link in the living chain which stretches unbroken from this present moment back to Jesus Christ. The glory of teaching is that it links the present with the earthly life of Jesus Christ."[2]

Today is our day. This is our time. Will we be giants and continue to be a link in the living chain of faithful men as God intended, or will we fail to mature?

Finally, be strong in the Lord and in the strength of His might. Put on the full armor of God, so that you will be able to stand firm against the schemes of the Devil. For our struggle is not against flesh and blood, but against the rulers, against the powers, against the world forces of this darkness, against the spiritual forces of wickedness in the heavenly places. Therefore, take up the full armor of God, so that you will be able to resist in the evil day, and having done everything, to stand firm. (Eph. 6:10–13)

Endnotes

Chapter 1: Standing in the Fire

1. Ken Jenkins is the source of the sequoia material and photos in this book. Ken has a book coming out soon about the sequoias, as well as a book with Warren Wiersbe about living a full life. For more information about Ken's ministry through photography and speaking, visit www.kenjenkins.com.

Chapter 2: Fireproof Your Life Right Now

1. "A Man You Would Write About" (song), by Billy Simon, copyright 1990, River Oaks Music Company, BMI, locally owned music, BMI. All rights administered by Meadowgreen Group, Nashville, TN.
2. Vance Havner, *Pepper and Salt* (Westwood, NJ: Fleming H. Revell, 1966), p. 9.

Chapter 3: Fireproof Your Faith

1. Ron Dunn, *The Faith Crisis* (Wheaton, IL: Tyndale, 1984), p. 14.
2. Adapted and condensed from Ron Dunn, p. 25.
3. All quotes from *The Complete Gathered Gold* (Darlington, UK: Evangelical Press, 2006).
4. Warren Wiersbe, *Bible Exposition Commentary* (Wheaton, IL: Victor Books, 1989), digital edition (CD).

Chapter 4: Fireproof Your Heart and Mind

1. Robert. D. Spender, article in *Evangelical Dictionary of Biblical Theology* (Grand Rapids, MI: Baker Books, 1996).
2. J.B. Lightfoot, *St. Paul's Epistles to the Colossians and to Philemon* (Grand Rapids, MI: Zondervan, 1959 [reprint of 1879 ed.]), p. 209.
3. Wiersbe, *Bible Exposition Commentary*.
4. A.T. Robertson, *Paul and the Intellectuals* (Nashville: Broadman, 1959), p. 98.
5. Wiersbe, *Bible Exposition Commentary*.
6. These points are borrowed from Bill Elliff's publication by Life Action Ministries, "Personal Revival Checklist." For more information, visit www.lifeaction.org.

Chapter 5: Fireproof Your Convictions

1. DJ Readers Report, *Discipleship Journal*, Issue 72 (Nov./Dec. 1992).
2. Chuck Swindoll, *The Finishing Touch* (Dallas, TX: Word, 1994), pp. 580-81.

Chapter 6: Fireproof Your Decision-Making

1. From an article by Good News Publishers, date unknown.
2. Gary Inrig, *Hearts of Iron, Feet of Clay* (Chicago: Moody Press, 1979), pp. 109–10.
3. Brother Lawrence, *The Practice of the Presence of God*, first letter.

Chapter 7: Fireproof Your Marriage

1. John Leo, "On Society," *U. S. News and World Report*, September 22, 1997, p. 14.

2. The purpose of this chapter is to save existing marriages, not to deal with marriages that are over. If, however, your marriage is already dissolved, my advice is this: If God allows you a second chance, go and sin no more. Don't carry the baggage of the past into your next relationship. Seek wise counsel. Don't blame the other party. Ask God what you could have done differently. Don't let marriage become a matter of trial and error.

3. Charles Swindoll, *Commitment: The Key To Marriage* (Portland, OR: Multnomah, 1981), p. 5.

4. Tertullian, *Ad Uxorem* (To My Wife), Book 2 (ca. 202 A.D.).

5. *New Man Magazine*, January/ February 1995.

6. Peter T. Kilborn, *New York Times*, June 1, 2005.

7. Charles Sell, *Achieving the Impossible: Intimate Marriage* (Portland, OR: Multnomah, 1982), p. 163.

8. Wiersbe, *Bible Exposition Commentary*.

9. James Dobson, as quoted in Bruce Barton, et al., *Life Application Commentary*, 1 Peter (Tyndale, 1996), digital edition.

Chapter 8: Fireproof Your Finances

1. Bill Bright, *As You Sow* (San Bernadino, CA: Here's Life Publishers, 1989), p. 62.

2. Bill Stafford, *The Adventure of Spirit-Filled Giving* (Zulon Press, 2007), pp. 39–40.

3. Wiersbe, *Bible Exposition Commentary*.

4. John Bisagno, *The Power of Positive Giving* (Nashville: Broadman Press, 1988), p. 42.

Chapter 9: Fireproofing for Times of Conflict and Crisis

1. Emmett C. Murphy, *The Genius of Sitting Bull: Thirteen Heroic Strategies for Today's Business Leaders* (Englewood Cliffs, NJ: Prentice Hall, 1992).
2. John Mason, *Why Ask Why? If You Know the Right Questions You Can Find the Right Answers* (Gainesville, FL: Bridge-Logos, 2000).
3. William R. Moody, *The Life of D.L. Moody* (New York: Macmillan, 1930), p. 131.
4. Adapted and condensed from George and Donald Sweeting, *Lessons from the Life of Moody* (Chicago: Moody Press, 1989), pp. 37–40.

Chapter 10: Fireproof Your Life for Eternity

1. *The Complete Gathered Gold*, p. 634.
2. Vance Havner, "Home Before Dark" (sermon).
3. Ibid.

Epilogue: Leaving a Legacy

1. For more information about the ministries of Ron Dunn and Vance Havner, visit www.rondunn.com and www.vancehavner.com to find books and resources to help you when you are going through the fire.
2. William Barclay, *The Letters to Timothy, Titus and Philemon* (Philadelphia: Westminster, 1957), p. 182.

This book was produced by CLC Publications. We hope it has been life-changing and has given you a fresh experience of God through the work of the Holy Spirit. CLC Publications is an outreach of CLC Ministries International, a global literature mission with work in over 50 countries. If you would like to know more about us or are interested in opportunities to serve with a faith mission, we invite you to contact us at:

CLC Ministries International
PO Box 1449
Fort Washington, PA 19034

—————

Phone: (215) 542-1242
E-mail: clcmail@clcusa.org
Website: www.clcusa.org

— —

DO YOU LOVE GOOD CHRISTIAN BOOKS?
Do you have a heart for worldwide missions?

You can receive a FREE subscription to
CLC's newsletter on global literature missions.

Order by e-mail at:

clcheartbeat@clcusa.org

or fill in the coupon below and mail to:

P.O. Box 1449
Fort Washington, PA 19034

┌ ─ ─ ─ ─ ─ ─ ─ ─ ─ ─ ─ ─ ─ ─ ─ ─ ─ ─ ─ ┐

FREE *HEARTBEAT* SUBSCRIPTION!

Name: _____

Address: _____

_____

Phone: _____ E-mail: _____

└ ─ ─ ─ ─ ─ ─ ─ ─ ─ ─ ─ ─ ─ ─ ─ ─ ─ ─ ─ ┘

READ THE REMARKABLE STORY OF
the founding of
CLC International

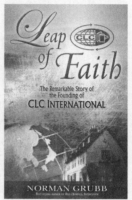

"Any who doubt that Elijah's God still lives ought to read of the money supplied when needed, the stores and houses provided, and the appearance of personnel in answer to prayer."

—Moody Monthly

Is it possible that the printing press, the editor's desk, the Christian bookstore, and the mail order department, can glow with the fast-moving drama of an "Acts of the Apostles"?

Find out, as you are carried from two people in an upstairs bookroom to a worldwide chain of Christian bookcenters, multiplied by nothing but a "shoestring" of faith and committed, though unlikely, lives.

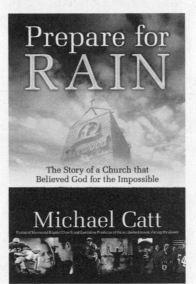

Prepare for Rain

A Story of a Church that Believed God for the Impossible

Michael Catt

Two farmers prayed for rain, but only one plowed his fields to receive it. *Which one are you?*

Only God can send revival, but there is much we can do to be ready when it comes. This was the lesson that Pastor Michael Catt and Sherwood Baptist Church discovered as God worked in them to help "reach the world from Albany, Georgia."

Follow the story of Pastor Catt and his congregation as the Lord changes a "typical Southern Baptist church" into a ministry center that reaches thousands through a variety of outreach programs, and has even challenged the Hollywood establishment with a locally produced, nationally syndicated movie, *Facing the Giants*.

Trade paper • 192 pages • 978-0-87508-977-5

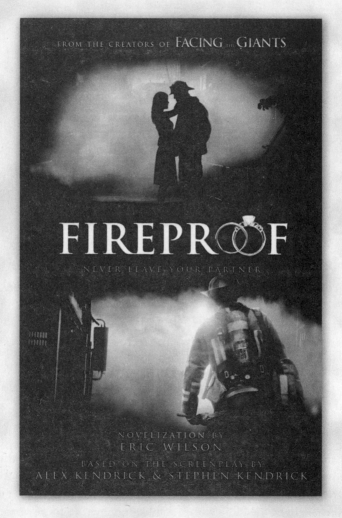

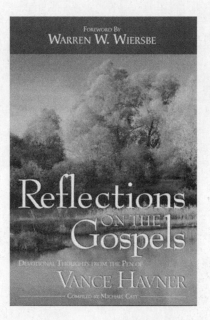

Reflections on the Gospels

Vance Havner

Rescued by Michael Catt from a collection of newspaper columns and compiled for the first time in book form, this wonderful devotional gives a unique insight into God's Word through the eyes of this great preacher.

Trade paper • 227 pages • 978-0-87508-783-2

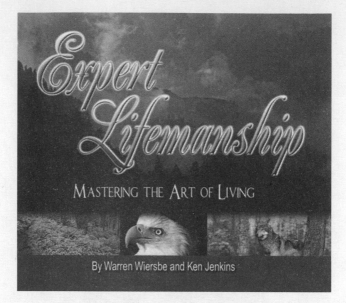

Expert Lifemanship

Warren Wiersbe & Ken Jenkins

Mastering the Art of Living

What do we do with life?

Sometimes life's crises, or even its predictability, can derail us from the path of God's purpose. He intends, however, that we live to the full. Learning to wait on Him for His overcoming strength will enable us "to rise up with wings as eagles, to run and not be weary, and to walk and not faint."

This grand theme is explored in the words of Warren Wiersbe, punctuated by the stunning nature photography of Ken Jenkins. What is created is an appealing invitation to get a new perspective on your existence in this world—and maybe change your life.

Full color photos and text

Coffee Table book • 112 pages • 978-0-87508-988-1